THE QUICK
CHOLESTEROL
& FAT
COUNTER™

THE QUICK CHOLESTEROL & FAT COUNTER™

By
Peter Cox and Peggy Brusseau

CENTURY

LONDON SYDNEY AUCKLAND JOHANNESBURG

Published by Random Century Ltd,
20 Vauxhall Bridge Road, London, SW1V 2SA

Random Century Australia (Pty) Ltd,
20 Alfred Street, Milsons Point, Sydney, NSW 2061
Australia

Random Century New Zealand Ltd,
18 Poland Road, Glenfield, Auckland 10,
New Zealand

Random Century South Africa (Pty) Ltd,
PO Box 337, Bergvlei 2012, South Africa

First published in 1989
Reprinted 1989, 1990 (three times), 1991

Set in Photina by Servis Filmsetting Ltd,
Richmond House, Richmond Grove, Longsight, Manchester

Printed and bound in Great Britain by
The Guernsey Press Co. Ltd, Guernsey, Channel Islands

British Library Cataloguing in Publication Data

Cox, Peter, 1955
The quick cholesterol and fat counter.
I. Title   II. Brusseau, Peggy
616.'05

ISBN 0–7126–3042–2

CONTENTS

	Page
Acknowledgements	6
Important Note	7
Welcome! to The Quick Cholesterol And Fat Counter™	9
Introducing The Quick Cholesterol Quotient	13
How to Use The Quick Cholesterol And Fat Counter™	15
How to Plan Your Daily Diet	19
The Quick Cholesterol Day-Planner	21
The Foods	23
Appendix I: Tracking Your Fat	154
Appendix II: How 'Cholesterol Quotients' Have Been Calculated	155

ACKNOWLEDGEMENTS

We would like to thank Neil Carr, Chris Esther and Peter Lofting for their assistance with data processing, Dr. S. B. Rosalki of the Department of Chemical Pathology, The Royal Free Hospital for his comments on the manuscript, and Sonia L. Connor of the section of clinical nutrition and lipid metabolism, Department of Medicine, The Oregon Health Sciences University for her kind permission to use the cholesterol/saturated fax index.

Back cover photograph by Carole Latimer

IMPORTANT NOTE

The recommendations made in this book are for adults only. If you suspect you may suffer from a raised cholesterol level, we strongly advise you to seek qualified medical treatment. Do not attempt self-treatment without first discussing and agreeing the proposed treatment with your doctor. Diagnosis and treatment of medical conditions is a responsibility shared between you and your doctor, and neither the authors nor publisher can accept responsibility for the consequences of treatment based on the recommendations described herein.

Proprietary Names

This book may include words, brand names and other descriptions of products which are or are asserted to be proprietary names or trademarks. No judgement concerning the legal status of such words is made or implied thereby. Their inclusion does not imply that they have acquired for legal purposes a non-proprietary or general significance nor any other judgement concerning their legal status.

The Quick Cholesterol Clean-Out™ and *The Quick Cholesterol and Fat Counter*™ are trademarks of The Quick Cholesterol Clean-Out Company Limited and may not be used for any purpose without express permission.

WELCOME!
TO
THE QUICK CHOLESTEROL AND
FAT COUNTER™

We've written this book for two sorts of people:
- First, for those intelligent folk who care enough about their health to want to keep their cholesterol levels within prudent limits. For you, this book will help you to choose good food, and shun the bad.
- And second, this book is also for those equally smart people who have succeeded in lowering their cholesterol levels, and who want to make sure they don't get out of hand again.

In our book *The Quick Cholesterol Clean-Out*™, we showed how you could take immediate steps to lower your cholesterol by natural dietary means. But eventually, all diets end, don't they? And then what do you do? Chances are, you'll be tempted to go back to your old ways of eating . . . and possibly undo all the good work you've achieved. We felt a special obligation to readers of *The Quick Cholesterol Clean-Out*™ because we *didn't* want to abandon you after all the hard work you've put in! So here's *The Quick Cholesterol and Fat Counter*™, with this important difference – this time, *you're* the boss. You don't have to follow someone else's idea of a good menu. *The Quick Cholesterol and Fat Counter*™ gives you the information you need to check your diet quickly and effortlessly, while allowing you to please your own culinary tastes from a vast range of foods. What could be better?

THE CHOLESTEROL TIMEBOMB

If you haven't read our previous book, you may be wondering why anyone needs to bother about his or her cholesterol level. Well, let's try and briefly explain what all the fuss is about. As you may know, we all *need* some cholesterol. Your body uses it to make hormones, bile and cell membranes. But you don't need very much, and that's where the problem begins. Because every day, your body manufactures about 1 gram of cholesterol, and takes in a further 0.5 gram from your diet. However, this is much more than you actually need – about four times as much, in fact. Now if your body doesn't process it properly, a little cholesterol will probably stick around in your system, slowly building up year by year, until eventually the level of cholesterol in your blood can become dangerously high – just like sediment builds up in a river.

Because it happens so slowly, you don't notice it. No one can *feel* their cholesterol level as it builds up, and even when an artery becomes more than half blocked by this fatty, cholesterol-rich sludge known as *atheroma*, you may still not be aware of any warning signs to tell you that something is badly wrong. In fact, an artery usually has to be more than 75 per cent blocked before blood flow is seriously impeded. But by this stage, time is definitely running out.

Our bodies depend on the normal flow of blood through minute capillaries, larger arteries (which transport oxygen-rich blood away from the heart) and veins (which carry blood back to the heart again) to nourish all our organs and body tissues, and this same remarkable system, consisting of thousands of kilometres of blood vessels, also helps to eliminate waste products. Every day, your heart will beat 100,000 times (2500 million times in a lifetime) as it provides the motive power to drive blood through this huge network of intricately connected vessels. Every minute, your heart circulates your body's entire volume of blood, about 5 litres, once round your system (pumping 200 million litres in a lifetime). If your heart stops beating for more than 3 minutes, permanent brain damage may occur. Being a hard-working muscle, the heart also supplies itself with vital oxygen and nourishment through its own pumping actions and again, if the blood flow through the life-giving coronary arteries is stopped for more than a few minutes, the heart will be damaged to such a great extent that it may be irreversibly stopped. So you see, when something happens to interrupt or diminish your blood flow, the situation can become very serious, very quickly.

As cholesterol sludge builds up on the walls of the arteries it begins to narrow them. If allowed to continue, this process will ultimately deprive vital organs of their blood supply, and you will die. The evidence shows that by the age of 65, 1 man in 5 has suffered a heart attack, and of these, 1 in 10 has died. But don't make the mistake of thinking that a high cholesterol level in your blood is only associated with heart disease. In fact, the same cholesterol sludge which forms deposits that build up on artery walls in the heart can also act to reduce the flow of blood in the brain causing what we commonly know as a 'stroke'. Most strokes are caused by a narrowing or blockage of an artery, leading to a 'cerebrovascular accident', involving damage to the brain. Of course, those who survive a heart attack or stroke – two types of cardiovascular ('heart and blood vessel') disease – *can* make a good recovery, if they are prepared to change their lifestyles sufficiently. But wouldn't it be more sensible to take *preventive* action now, rather than fighting for your life later on?

Of course it would. And that's why every sensible person will get to know their cholesterol level (do *you* know yours yet?) and take appropriate action if it's too high.* But what, exactly, *is* 'too high'? Here's a guide:

For information on how to find out what your cholesterol level is (and on other aspects of cholesterol and health), see our book The Quick Cholesterol Clean-Out.

CHECK OUT YOUR CHOLESTEROL LEVEL

5.2 mmols/litre or less

The desirable level. Do not make adverse changes to your lifestyle (smoking, fatty foods, lack of exercise, excessive stress). Take another test in 5 years' time.

5.2 to 6.2 mmols/litre

Borderline high. Follow cholesterol-reduction programme and take cholesterol tests annually. If you also smoke, have high blood pressure or are obese, cut out these risks. Some further testing may be necessary.

Over 6.2 mmols/litre

High. Follow cholesterol-reduction programme and cut out other risk factors. If no success, drug treatment may be necessary.

(Adapted from guidelines issued by the US National Heart, Lung and Blood Institute)

Sometimes you will find cholesterol measured in milligrams per decilitre (abbreviated to mg/dl). These values can be converted to millimoles (mmols) per litre by dividing by 38.66.

But is it worth trying to reduce your cholesterol level if it's too high? Yes, most definitely. You see, we know from extensive observations involving thousands of people that if a high cholesterol level is reduced, your chances of leading a long, healthy life greatly improve. Indeed, there's a simple little formula which scientists have calculated:

For every 1 per cent drop in blood cholesterol, there is a 2 per cent drop in the risk of cardiovascular disease.

Think about this for a moment. It means that, when a population manages to reduce its cholesterol level by, say, a meagre 5 per cent, the risk of cardiovascular disease drops by 10 per cent. And if the level of cholesterol declines by 10 per cent, then the risk drops by 20 per cent, and so on. Now, of course, this fact has profound implications for all of us. It means that reducing our blood cholesterol level is one of the most effective ways yet discovered to *dramatically reduce* our risk of suffering from – or being killed by – cardiovascular disease. And if you also take prompt action to eliminate or reduce other risk factors (shown below) then you can be sure that you're doing your utmost to really look after that body of yours!

FOUR WAYS TO CUT YOUR RISK

Smoking

Stub it out, before it stubs you out. According to Professor Julian Peto of the Institute of Cancer Research, the only thing that persuades more than 50% of smokers to give up is having a heart attack. So get ahead of the game and quit while you're ahead – better still, don't start.

High blood pressure

Get your blood pressure checked. Cut down on the salt you eat, lose weight, cut down on alcohol. And learn how to relax – stress can be a killer.

Obesity

A high blood cholesterol level occurs more than twice as often in the overweight than in the non-overweight . . . even an excess of only 5 lb can threaten your health. Try pinching the skin under your upper arm. Slightly more than 2.5 cm (1 in) thickness of skin is acceptable for a man, slightly less than one inch for a woman. More than this, and you may need to lose weight.

Lack of exercise

Studies show that women who don't exercise are three times more likely to die of a heart attack than those who stay in shape. Exercise combined with dieting may be the most effective way to lose weight and keep it off, and it protects against heart disease.

INTRODUCING THE QUICK CHOLESTEROL QUOTIENT

Now let's shatter one central myth about cholesterol. *The amount of cholesterol in your blood* doesn't *just depend on the amount of cholesterol in your diet*. You see, the problem with simply measuring the amount of cholesterol you eat in your food is that it only tells you part of the story. In fact, the level of cholesterol in your body depends on *both the amount of cholesterol and the amount of saturated fat you eat*. It's a complicated relationship, but of the two, the amount of saturated fat you consume probably affects your cholesterol level more dramatically than the amount of cholesterol you eat! Confusing? Well, we don't think so, because help is at hand in the form of your very own 'Cholesterol Quotient'.

Using the 'Cholesterol Quotient' (let's call it 'the CQ' for short) is rather like having a personal bodyguard. Its sole purpose in life is to protect you by preventing you from eating food which is likely to raise your cholesterol level. At the same time, it will show you all the food you *can* eat and enjoy safely.

Until recently, no one could really say for sure how 'good' or 'bad' different foods were likely to be for your long-suffering arteries. Then some clever university researchers in Portland, Oregon confronted this problem, and after much medical and mathematical work, they produced a scoring system that would allow anyone quickly and simply to compare different types of food for their ability to raise your cholesterol level and block up your blood vessels. Using this formula, we've calculated CQs for all the foods in this book. To put it simply, the CQ gives you a good idea of just how good – or bad – eating a certain food is likely to be for you. Remember:

The lower *the CQ rating, the* better *it is.*

The higher *the CQ rating, the* worse *it is.*

Yes, it's just like counting calories, but with this very important difference: Using the CQ rating to help you choose foods wisely will actually help you to improve the *quality* of the food you eat. And that's something that just counting calories can never do.

SETTING YOUR OWN CQ LIMIT

So what should your maximum CQ limit be each day? Well, different people will have different limits, depending on their existing cholesterol level, the type of medication they may be taking, and the efficiency with which their bodies can process the cholesterol in their systems. Only you and your medical advisors can decide upon the CQ limit that is most appropriate for your own circumstances. However, here are some general guidelines (more information about these calculations is given in Appendix II):

CQ Limit 1 : For the general population

40 CQs per day. In general, no one (whether or not they have a cholesterol problem) should exceed this limit.

CQ Limit 2: For those with some risk factors

30 CQs per day. If your present cholesterol level is 6.2 mmols/litre OR above OR if your cholesterol level is 5.2 mmols/litre or above *and* you suffer from coronary heart disease *or* have associated risk factors, then use this limit. The recommendations of an expert committee of the World Health Organization on the prevention of heart disease also suggest that a great many other people should also keep within the intakes represented by Limit 2.

CQ Limit 3: For those with a greater need to lower cholesterol

20 CQs a day. If you have tried CQ Limit 2 for about three months but cholesterol-lowering is insufficient, you may then wish to reduce further your saturated fat and cholesterol intake to this level.

These limits are, of course, generalizations, and should be modified on the advice of your doctor or dietician. Now you've discovered your personal 'Sludge Limit', you'll want to start putting it to good use. Well, we have provided a convenient day-planning form on page 21 for you to use as you keep track of your daily food intake. And remember – make sure that your total daily intake *doesn't* exceed your limit.

HOW TO USE
THE QUICK CHOLESTEROL AND
FAT COUNTER™

Using this book is simplicity itself. You'll be amazed how easy it is to find the right food, straight away. Make sure that you take the book along when you're eating out – it'll be your guide as you navigate through restaurant menus. And remember to take it to the supermarket when you're shopping, because it works just as well there, too.

The foods are arranged in alphabetical order, so you should be able to find what you want immediately – for example, to look up 'marmalade', look under the Ms, and to look up 'Yorkshire pudding', look under the Ys. Some foods are gathered together under a main heading, because it makes better sense to keep them all together; this allows you to look at similar foods within a group and see how their CQ ratings compare. The main food groups are:

Alcohol	Margarine
Beans and Pulses	Milk
Beef	Nut and Seed Butters
Biscuits	Nuts
Bread	Oil
Breakfast Cereals	Pies
Cakes	Pork
Carbonated Drinks	Potatoes
Cereals and Grain	Puddings
Cheese	Rice
Chicken	Salad Dressings
Chocolate	Salads
Duck	Sandwiches
Eggs	Sauces
Fat	Sausages
Fish and Shellfish	Seeds and Seed Products
Flour	Soup
Goose	Spices
Gravy	Sweets
Lamb	Turkey
Luncheon Meat	Veal

For example, to look up 'tomato soup', you would look under 'Soup' until you found the type of tomato soup you were thinking about buying or eating. You will see four columns of figures on each page. It's the *last* column that gives you the CQ rating for each food. Choose the food with the *lowest* CQ rating – and that's it! (For information about the three other figures, see Appendix I).

WHAT ELSE CAN YOU DO?

Apart from keeping tabs on your cholesterol and saturated fat intake, you can also make a special effort to eat those kinds of food which are known to have a cholesterol-lowering effect by themselves (explained more fully in our book *The Quick Cholesterol Clean-Out*™). Some of them are:

Oats and oat products (but *without* any added fat; this excludes most brands of oatcakes).

Corn bran   Not widely available yet, but worth trying to find. (It is included in products such as polenta.)

Beans and pulses   Particularly green beans, kidney beans, haricot beans, pinto beans, and good old humble baked beans. All of them can lower cholesterol quite remarkably if taken on a daily basis.

Guar gum   Made from the ground-up seed of the tree *Cyamopsis tetragonolobus*, and often used to bind pills and tablets. It has also been used as a 'slimming pill', intended to be taken with water because it swells up in the stomach thus producing a feeling of fullness and, hopefully, a decreased appetite. However, there have been safety fears about its use in this manner, since guar gum could swell up in the gullet causing a dangerous obstruction.

Pectin   Made from apples or citrus fruits. It is the gelling agent used to make fruit jams and jellies.

Psyllium seeds   Again, some adverse reactions have been noted following psyllium usage, including allergic reaction (anaphylaxis) and hypersensitivity leading to anaphylactic shock. Best to check with your doctor.

'Beta fibre'   A completely new fibre product, made from the residue of sugar beet after the sugar has been extracted. Like other dry fibre supplements, it should not be consumed in its raw state but should first be moistened and time given to allow it to swell; otherwise it can stick in the gullet.

A NOTE ABOUT THE FOODS

We have tried to include a good selection of the common and not-so-common (especially ethnic) foods that people eat, and we've also tried to make this book as easy to use as possible. Please let us know if you have any comments, or would like to make any suggestions for future editions. An address to which you can write can be found at the end of the book.

In some cases, it simply has not been possible to obtain reliable information for some kinds of food. We have, however, included information for many different kinds of 'raw' food (indicated by italics), which will allow you to calculate your own CQ ratings for a recipe or dish which is not included here. Where a dish has been analysed (for example, hot pot), it should be understood that there are many individual ways of preparing it, each involving differing amounts of fat and cholesterol, and therefore our figures can only be an approximate guide. For the sake of clarity, figures have been rounded to the nearest whole number.

A NOTE ABOUT CALORIES

By reducing your intake of fatty foods, you will automatically be reducing the number of calories you take in your diet, because fat is the greatest single source of calories. However, don't forget that calories still count. Alcohol, for example, generally has 'zero' ratings in the tables that follow, because it contains no saturated fat or cholesterol, but is still a significant source of calories. Alcohol and other sugars may raise the body's production of insulin, a hormone which stimulates the manufacture of fats called triglycerides. These fatty substances are, like cholesterol, both taken in with food and manufactured in the liver. They are used by the body to provide energy, and help us to store fat in our fat tissues. But triglycerides are not free from suspicion in coronary heart disease. As we eat more food containing triglycerides, it has been found that the rate of cholesterol absorption increases. Also, since they have an effect on blood clotting, someone with high triglyceride levels and with artery-narrowing athero-sclerosis could suffer from a blocked artery due to a blood clot. A raised triglyceride level is usually treated in the first instance by counting calories and losing weight (if necessary), by taking regular exercise and by cutting out alcohol. So remember, especially if you have a raised triglyceride level or if you have a weight problem, your calorie intake is still important.

HOW TO PLAN YOUR DAILY DIET

It's not only easy but also great fun to plan out a day's menu, and it certainly teaches you what sorts of food you can eat freely, and which ones you'd be better off avoiding. Let's take you through one day's menu-planning step by step . . .

First, you have to find out what your personal CQ Limit is. In this example, let's assume that Limit 2 applies – that is, 30 CQs per day. Let's start with breakfast . . .

A 'typical' breakfast menu probably consists of coffee, corn flakes and orange juice. So add up the CQs for each item, not forgetting to include the (low-fat) milk on the cornflakes.

	CQ rating
1 cup coffee (black)	0
1 bowl corn flakes with milk	7
1 cup orange juice	0

So far, so good. Your running CQ total is 7. Now for a mid-morning snack – perhaps

1 low-fat yoghurt	3

Lunches can be a problem if you're a busy, working person. There's usually no time to prepare your own food, and so you have to depend on the food you can buy locally. A baked potato is one of those foods you can buy just about everywhere, so try:

1 baked potato	0
1 cup baked beans	0

Remember, if you add a pat of butter or margarine to that baked potato, you're going to increase your CQ total by about 3. For a mid-afternoon snack, you might like to consider:

1 cup tea made with $\frac{1}{4}$ cup milk	2

And for a little variety, how about having a packet of raisins and pumpkin seeds handy to munch whenever you feel the need:

1 oz pumpkin seeds	2
2 oz raisins	0

Now for dinner, you'll probably want something hot and substantial, so try macaroni cheese, but try making it with margarine rather than butter (less saturated fat).

$1\frac{1}{2}$ cups macaroni cheese. 11
1 cup cooked spinach 0
$\frac{1}{2}$ cup boiled carrots. 0

Overall, your CQ total is 25, well within your daily limit of 30. So you see, it's not too difficult to plan a good day's diet which gives you all the nutrition you need, but which doesn't exceed your CQ Limit!

THE QUICK CHOLESTEROL DAY-PLANNER

Use this form (or copies) to plan out your day's diet. . .

FOOD   **CQ RATING**

Breakfast

. . . .
. . . .
. . . .
. . . .
. . . .

Lunch

. . . .
. . . .
. . . .
. . . .
. . . .

Dinner

. . . .
. . . .
. . . .
. . . .
. . . .

Snacks

. . . .
. . . .
. . . .
. . . .
. . . .
. . . .

TOTAL DAY'S CQ: . . . .

YOUR PERSONAL CQ LIMIT: . . . .
Did you keep within it? If your day's intake is less than your CQ limit, congratulations! If not, plan it again.

THE

FOODS

	TOTAL FAT (g)	SATURATED FAT (g)	CHOLES- TEROL (mg)	CQ
ALCOHOL				
Beer				
Bitter and Stout, ½ Pint (285ml)	0	0	0	0
Lager, ½ Pint (285ml)	0	0	0	0
Bloody Mary				
1 Glass	0	0	0	0
Champagne				
1 Glass	0	0	0	0
Cider				
½ Pint (285ml)	0	0	0	0
Creme de Menthe, 36% Vol				
1 Glass	0	0	0	0
Daiquiri				
1 Glass	0	0	0	0
1 Tin	0	0	0	0
Fortified Wines (Port, Sherry)				
1 Glass	0	0	0	0
Gin and Tonic				
1 Glass	0	0	0	0
Gin Fizz				
1 Glass	0	0	0	0
Liqueur				
Coffee with Cream, 17% Vol, 1 Measure	7	5	7	5
Coffee, 26.5% Vol, 1 Measure	0	0	0	0
Coffee, 31.5% Vol, 1 Measure	0	0	0	0
Manhattan Cocktail				
1 Glass	0	0	0	0
Martini Cocktail				
1 Glass	0	0	0	0
Pina Colada				
1 Glass	3	1	0	1
1 Tin	17	15	0	15
Spirits (Brandy, Gin, Rum, Vodka, Whisky)				
1 Measure	0	0	0	0
Whisky and Soda				
1 Glass	0	0	0	0
Wine				
Dessert, Dry, 1 Glass	0	0	0	0
Dessert, Sweet, 1 Glass	0	0	0	0
Table, All, 1 Glass	0	0	0	0
Alfalfa Seeds				
Sprouted, Fresh, 1 Cup (33g)	0	0	0	0
Almonds				
Dried, 1 Cup Kernels (142g)	74	7	0	7
Dry Roasted, 1 Cup Kernels (138g)	71	7	0	7

	TOTAL FAT (g)	SATURATED FAT (g)	CHOLES- TEROL (g)	CO (mg)
Apple Juice				
Frozen Concentrate, Diluted, 1 Glass	0	0	0	0
Frozen Concentrate, Undiluted, 6 Fl.oz Container (211g)	1	0	0	0
Tinned or Bottled, 1 Glass	0	0	0	0
Apple sauce				
Tinned, 1 Cup (255g)	1	0	0	0
Apples				
Dried, Stewed, 1 Cup (280g)	0	0	0	0
Dried, Uncooked, 1 Cup (86g)	0	0	0	0
Frozen Rings, 1 Cup (206g)	1	0	0	0
Raw, with Skin, 1 Fruit	1	0	0	0
Raw, without Skin, 1 Fruit	0	0	0	0
Tinned, 1 Cup (204g)	1	0	0	0
Apricot Nectar				
Tinned or Bottled, 1 Glass (251g)	0	0	0	0
Apricots				
Dried, Stewed, 1 Cup (270g)	0	0	0	0
Dried, Uncooked, 1 Cup (130g)	1	0	0	0
Frozen, 1 Cup (242g)	0	0	0	0
Fresh, 3 Fruits	0	0	0	0
Tinned, 1 Cup (248g)	0	0	0	0
Arrowroot				
Boiled, 1 Piece (12g)	0	0	0	0
Fresh, 1 Piece (12g)	0	0	0	0
Artichokes				
Globe, Boiled, 1 Med Artichoke (120g)	0	0	0	0
Globe, Boiled, ½ Cup Hearts (84g)	0	0	0	0
Jerusalem, Boiled, 1 Cup Slices (150g)	0	0	0	0
Asparagus				
Boiled, 4 Spears (60g)	0	0	0	0
Tinned, Drained Solids, 1 Tin (248g)	2	0	0	0
Tinned, Solids and Liquid, 1 Tin (411g)	1	0	0	0
Aubergine				
Boiled or Baked, 1 Cup Cubes (96g)	0	0	0	0
Fried in Butter, 1 Cup Cubes (96g) and 1 oz Butter	23	14	62	18
Fried in Margarine, 1 Cup, Cubes (96g) and 1 oz Margarine	23	4	0	4

	TOTAL FAT (g)	SATURATED FAT (g)	CHOLES- TEROL (mg)	CO
Fried in Oil, 1 Cup Cubes (96g) and 2 Tablespoons Oil	27	2	0	2
Avocado Dip – *See* Guacamole				
Avocado and Prawn Cocktail				
1 Fruit, Prawns (64g) and Dressing	54	8	127	15
Avocado Vinaigrette				
1 Fruit and Vinaigrette with Olive Oil	39	6	0	6
Avocados				
Fresh, 1 Fruit	31	5	0	5
Bacon				
Cured, Tinned, 3.5oz (100g)	72	23	89	28
Long Back, Grilled, 2 Slices (46.5g)	4	1	27	3
Long Back, Raw, 2 Slices (56.7g)	4	1	28	3
Streaky, Grilled, Shallow-fried or Roasted, 3 Medium Slices (19g)	9	3	16	4
Streaky, Raw, 3 Medium Slices (68g)	39	15	46	17
Top Back, Grilled or Roasted, 3 Raw Slices (34g)	13	4	36	6
Top Back, Raw, 3 Slices (68g)	25	9	47	11
Bacon Substitute, Meatless				
1 Strip (8g)	2	0	0	0
1 Cup (144g)	43	7	0	7
Bagels				
Plain, 1 Bagel	1	0	0	0
Baked Beans *See under* Beans and Pulses				
Baked Potato				
See also under Potato				
1 Medium	0	0	0	0
1 Medium with ½ Tin (220g) Baked Beans	1	0	0	0
1 Medium with 1 Pat Butter	4	3	11	3
1 Medium with ½ Cup Low-fat Cottage Cheese	2	1	10	2
1 Medium with 1 Pat Butter and 55g Cheddar	23	15	71	18
Baking Powder				
1 Tbsp (9.5g)	0	0	0	0
Balsam-pear				
Boiled, 1 Cup (58g)	0	0	0	0
Fresh, ½ Cup (24g)	0	0	0	0

	TOTAL FAT (g)	SATURATED FAT (g)	CHOLES-TEROL (mg)	CQ
Bamboo Shoots				
Boiled, 1 Cup Slices (120g)	0	0	0	0
Tinned, 1 Tin (262g)	1	0	0	0
Fresh, 1 Cup Slices (151g)	1	0	0	0
Bananas				
Dehydrated or Banana Flakes, 1 Tbsp (6.2g)	0	0	0	0
1 Cup (100g)	2	1	0	1
Fresh, 1 Fruit	1	0	0	0
Barley, Pearl, Pot or Scotch				
1 Cup (200g)	2	0	0	0

BEANS AND PULSES

	TOTAL FAT (g)	SATURATED FAT (g)	CHOLES-TEROL (mg)	CQ
Aduki Beans				
1 Cup Boiled (230g)	0	0	0	0
1 Cup Tinned (296g)	0	0	0	0
Yokan, 3 Slices (43g)	0	0	0	0
Baked Beans				
Home Recipe with Pork, 1 Cup (253g)	13	5	13	6
Tinned, Plain or Vegetarian, 1 Cup (254g)	1	0	0	0
Tinned, with Beef, 1 Cup (266g)	9	5	59	7
Tinned, with Pork, 1 Cup (253g)	4	2	18	2
Tinned, with Sausages, 1 Cup (257g)	17	6	15	7
2 Slices Buttered Toast and 1 Tin (440g) Beans	12	6	22	7
2 Toast with Margarine and 1 Tin (440g) Beans	11	1	0	1
Beansprouts				
Stir-Fried, 1 Cup (124g)	0	0	0	0
Tinned, 1 Cup (125g)	0	0	0	0
Mixed, Fresh, ½ Cup (52g)	0	0	0	0
12oz Package (340g)	1	0	0	0
Bengal Gram – *See* Chickpeas				
Black Beans				
Boiled, 1 Cup (172g)	1	0	0	0
Black-eyed Beans				
Boiled, 1 Cup (171g)	1	0	0	0
Borlotti Beans				
Boiled, 1 Cup (169g)	1	0	0	0
British Field Beans				
Boiled, 1 Cup (177g)	1	0	0	0
Tinned, 1 Cup (262g)	1	0	0	0
Broadbeans				
Boiled, 1 Cup (170g)	1	0	0	0
Tinned, 1 Cup (256g)	1	0	0	0
Butter Beans				
Boiled, 1 Cup (188g)	1	0	0	0
Tinned, 1 Cup (241g)	0	0	0	0

	TOTAL FAT (g)	SATURATED FAT (g)	CHOLES- TEROL (mg)	CQ
Cannellini Beans				
Boiled, 1 Cup (179g)	1	0	0	0
Chickpeas				
Boiled, 1 Cup (164g)	4	0	0	0
Hummus, Home Recipe, 1 Cup (246g)	21	3	0	3
Tinned, 1 Cup (240g)	3	0	0	0
Dwarf Beans				
Boiled, 1 Cup (182g)	1	0	0	0
Flageolet Beans				
Boiled, 1 Cup (177g)	1	0	0	0
Tinned, 1 Cup (260g)	1	0	0	0
French Beans				
Boiled, 1 Cup (177g)	1	0	0	0
Ful Medames				
Boiled, 1 Cup (87g)	0	0	0	0
Garbanzo Beans – *See* Chickpeas				
Gram – *See* Chickpeas				
Haricot Beans				
Boiled, 1 Cup (182g)	1	0	0	0
Sprouted, Fresh, 1 Cup (104g)	1	0	0	0
Tinned, 1 Cup (262g)	1	0	0	0
Kidney Beans				
Boiled, 1 Cup (177g)	1	0	0	0
Sprouted, Fresh, 1 Cup (184g)	1	0	0	0
Tinned, 1 Cup (256g)	1	0	0	0
Lentils				
Boiled, 1 Cup (198g)	1	0	0	0
Dhal, Home Recipe, 1 Cup (210g)	15	2	0	2
Sprouted, Fresh, 1 Cup (77g)	0	0	0	0
Sprouted, Stir-fried, 3.5oz (100g)	1	0	0	0
Lima Beans				
Boiled, 1 Cup (170g)	1	0	0	0
Tinned, 1 Cup (248g)	1	0	0	0
Mixed White Beans				
Boiled, 1 Cup (179g)	1	0	0	0
Tinned, 1 Cup (262g)	1	0	0	0
Mung Beans				
Boiled, 1 Cup (202g)	1	0	0	0
Sprouted, Boiled, 1 Cup (124g)	0	0	0	0
Sprouted, Fresh, 1 Cup (100g)	0	0	0	0
Sprouted, Stir-fried, 1 Cup (124g)	0	0	0	0
Sprouted, Tinned, 1 Cup (125g)	0	0	0	0
Navy Beans				
Boiled, 1 Cup (172g)	10	1	0	1
Pigeon Peas				
Boiled, 1 Cup (168g)	1	0	0	0

	TOTAL FAT (g)	SATURATED FAT (g)	CHOLES-TEROL (mg)	CQ
Pinto Beans				
Boiled, 1 Cup (171g)	1	0	0	0
Tinned, 1 Cup (240g)	1	0	0	0
Red Gram – *See* Pigeon Peas				
Refried Beans				
Tinned, 1 Cup (253g)	3	1	0	1
Runner Beans				
Boiled, 1 Cup (125g)	0	0	0	0
Tinned, 1 Cup (135g)	0	0	0	0
Soybeans				
Boiled, 1 Cup (172g)	15	2	0	2
Dry Roasted, 1 Cup (172g)	37	5	0	5
Roasted, 1 Cup (172g)	44	6	0	6
Sprouted, Fresh, ½ Cup (35g)	2	0	0	0
Sprouted, Steamed, 1 Cup (94g)	4	1	0	0
Sprouted, Stir-fried, 3.5oz (100g)	7	1	0	0
Urd Beans				
Boiled, 1 Cup (180g)	1	0	0	0
Winged Beans				
Boiled, 1 Cup (62g)	0	0	0	0
Yardlong Beans				
Boiled, 1 Cup Slices (104g)	0	0	0	0
Yellow Snap Beans				
Boiled, 1 Cup (177g)	2	1	0	0

BEEF
See also under Luncheon Meat, Steak

Carcass: Whole

	TOTAL FAT (g)	SATURATED FAT (g)	CHOLES-TEROL (mg)	CQ
Choice Cuts, Lean and Fat, Raw, 1 lb (453.6g)	110	46	336	63
Composite of Trimmed Cuts				
Lean and Fat, Cooked, 3oz (85g)	23	10	77	13
Lean and Fat, Raw, 1 lb (453.6g)	107	46	318	62
Lean, Cooked, 3oz (85g)	9	3	77	7
Lean, Raw, 1 lb (453.6g)	29	11	272	25
Fat Trimmed from Retail Cuts				
Cooked, 3oz (85g)	60	25	81	30
Raw, 4oz (113g)	80	35	112	41
Good Cuts, Lean and Fat, Raw, 1 lb (453.6g)	104	44	336	61

Carcass: Parts

	TOTAL FAT (g)	SATURATED FAT (g)	CHOLES-TEROL (mg)	CQ
Arm Pot Roast				
Lean and Fat, Braised, 3oz (85g)	22	9	84	13
Lean and Fat, Raw, 1 lb (453.6g)	90	38	313	54
Lean, Braised, 3oz (85g)	9	3	86	8
Lean, Raw, 1 lb (453.6g)	23	9	272	22

	TOTAL FAT (g)	SATURATED FAT (g)	CHOLES- TEROL (mg)	CQ
Blade Roast				
Lean and Fat, Braised, 3oz (85g)	26	11	88	15
Lean and Fat, Raw, 1 lb (453.6g)	107	46	331	63
Lean, Braised, 3oz (85g)	13	5	90	10
Lean, Raw, 1 lb (453.6g)	41	16	295	31
Brain				
Shallow-fried, 3oz (85g)	14	3	1696	88
Simmered, 3oz (85g)	11	3	1746	90
Raw, 1 lb (452g)	42	10	7560	388

Brisket
Flat Half				
Lean and Fat, Braised, 3oz (85g)	30	12	78	16
Lean and Fat, Raw, 1 lb (453.6g)	144	61	345	79
Lean, Braised, 3oz (85g)	14	5	77	9
Lean, Raw, 1 lb (453.6g)	44	17	290	31
Lean and Fat, Braised, 3oz (85g)	25	10	81	14
Lean and Fat, Raw, 1 lb (453.6g)	111	47	322	64
Lean, Braised, 3oz (85g)	7	3	81	7
Point Half				
Lean, Raw, 1 lb (453.6g)	22	7	268	21
Whole				
Lean and Fat, Braised, 3oz (85g)	28	11	79	15
Lean and Fat, Raw, 1 lb (453.6g)	128	54	336	71
Lean, Braised, 3oz (85g)	11	4	79	8
Lean, Raw, 1 lb (453.6g)	33	11	277	25
Calf				
Heart, Braised, 1 Cup Chopped (145g)	13	7	397	27
Liver, Fried, 3oz Slice (85g)	11	3	372	21
Sweetbreads, Braised, 3oz (85g)	3	1	396	21
Sweetbreads, Raw, 3.5oz (100g)	2	1	250	14
Tongue, Braised, 1 Slice (20g)	1	1	20	2
Tongue, Raw, 3.5oz (100g)	5	3	70	7

Chuck
Blade				
Lean and Fat, Braised, 3oz (85g)	26	11	88	15
Lean and Fat, Raw, 1 lb (453.6g)	107	46	331	63
Lean, Braised, 3oz (85g)	13	5	90	10
Lean, Raw, 1 lb (453.6g)	41	16	295	31
Roast				
Lean and Fat, Braised, 3oz (85g)	22	9	84	13
Lean and Fat, Raw, 1 lb (453.6g)	90	38	313	54
Lean, Braised, 3oz (85g)	9	3	86	8
Lean, Raw, 1 lb (453.6g)	23	9	272	22

	TOTAL FAT (g)	SATURATED FAT (g)	CHOLES- TEROL (mg)	CQ
Corned Beef				
Brisket, Cooked, 3oz (85g)	16	5	83	10
Brisket, Raw, 1 lb (453.6g)	68	22	245	34
Dripping				
1 Tbsp (12.8g)	13	6	14	7
1 Cup (205g)	205	102	224	114
Flank				
Lean and Fat, Braised, 3oz (85g)	13	6	61	9
Lean and Fat, Grilled, 3oz (85g)	14	6	60	9
Lean and Fat, Raw, 1 lb (453.6g)	57	26	236	38
Lean, Braised, 3oz (85g)	12	5	60	8
Lean, Grilled, 3oz (85g)	13	5	60	8
Lean, Raw, 1 lb (453.6g)	43	18	227	30
Kidneys				
Simmered, 3oz (85g)	3	1	329	17
Raw 1 lb (452g)	14	4	1288	69
Liver				
Braised, 3oz (85g)	4	2	331	18
Shallow-fried, 3oz (85g)	7	2	410	23
Raw, 1 lb (452g)	17	7	1600	87

Mince

	TOTAL FAT (g)	SATURATED FAT (g)	CHOLES- TEROL (mg)	CQ
Lean				
Baked, Medium, 3oz (85g)	16	6	66	10
Baked, Well Done, 3oz (85g)	16	6	84	10
Grilled, Medium, 3oz (85g)	16	6	74	10
Grilled, Well Done, 3oz (85g)	15	6	86	10
Shallow-fried, Medium, 3oz (85g)	16	6	71	10
Shallow-fried, Well Done, 3oz (85g)	15	6	81	10
Raw, 4oz (113g)	23	9	85	14
Raw, 1 lb (452g)	93	38	340	55
Regular				
Baked, Medium, 3oz (85g)	18	7	74	11
Baked, Well Done, 3oz (85g)	18	7	92	12
Grilled, Medium, 3oz (85g)	18	7	77	11
Grilled, Well Done, 3oz (85g)	17	7	86	11
Shallow-fried, Medium, 3oz (85g)	19	8	76	11
Shallow-fried, Well Done, 3oz (85g)	16	6	83	11
Raw, 4oz (113g)	30	12	96	17
Raw, 1 lb (452g)	120	49	384	68
Porterhouse Steak				
Lean and Fat, Grilled, 3oz (85g)	18	8	71	11

	TOTAL FAT (g)	SATURATED FAT (g)	CHOLES-TEROL (mg)	CQ
Lean and Fat, Raw, 1 lb (453.6g)	106	45	318	61
Lean, Grilled, 3oz (85g)	9	4	68	7
Lean, Raw, 1 lb (453.6g)	36	14	272	28

Rib
Large End
Lean and Fat, Grilled, 3oz (85g)	28	12	74	15
Lean and Fat, Roasted, 3oz (85g)	26	11	72	14
Lean and Fat, Raw, 1 lb (453.6g)	142	62	331	79
Lean, Grilled, 3oz (85g)	12	5	70	9
Lean, Roasted, 3oz (85g)	12	5	69	8
Lean, Raw, 1 lb (453.6g)	43	19	268	32

Small End
Lean and Fat, Grilled, 3oz (85g)	21	9	71	13
Lean and Fat, Roasted, 3oz (85g)	25	11	72	14
Lean and Fat, Raw, 1 lb (453.6g)	118	51	318	67
Lean, Grilled, 3oz (85g)	10	4	68	7
Lean, Roasted, 3oz (85g)	12	5	68	8
Lean, Raw, 1 lb (453.6g)	37	15	268	29

Whole
Lean and Fat, Grilled, 3oz (85g)	26	11	73	15
Lean and Fat, Roasted, 3oz (85g)	27	11	72	15
Lean and Fat, Raw, 1 lb (453.6g)	132	57	327	74
Lean, Grilled, 3oz (85g)	11	5	70	8
Lean, Roasted, 3oz (85g)	12	5	69	8
Lean, Raw, 1 lb (453.6g)	41	17	268	31

Roast Beef
See also under individual cuts
Frozen Dinner, with Potatoes, Peas and Sweetcorn, 1 Serving (100g)	3	2	50	5
Home Recipe, 1 Portion	26	11	72	14
Tinned, 3.5oz (100g)	13	5	80	9

Round
Bottom Round
Lean and Fat, Braised, 3oz (85g)	13	5	82	9
Lean and Fat, Raw, 1 lb (453.6g)	71	29	295	44
Lean, Braised, 3oz (85g)	8	3	82	7
Lean, Raw, 1 lb (453.6g)	28	10	268	23

Eye of Round
Lean and Fat, Roasted, 3oz (85g)	12	5	62	8
Lean and Fat, Raw, 1 lb (453.6g)	57	24	272	38
Lean, Roasted, 3oz (85g)	6	2	59	5
Lean, Raw, 1 lb (453.6g)	19	7	245	19

Full Cut
Choice, Lean and Fat, Grilled, 3oz (85g)	16	6	71	10
Choice, Lean and Fat, Raw, 1 lb (453.6g)	80	34	299	49

	TOTAL FAT (g)	SATURATED FAT (g)	CHOLES- TEROL (mg)	CU
Choice, Lean, Grilled, 3oz (85g)	7	3	70	6
Choice, Lean, Raw, 1 lb (453.6g)	22	8	263	21
Tip Round				
Lean and Fat, Roasted, 3oz (85g)	13	5	71	9
Lean and Fat, Raw, 1 lb (453.6g)	62	26	295	41
Lean, Roasted, 3oz (85g)	6	2	69	6
Lean, Raw, 1 lb (453.6g)	20	7	272	21
Top Round				
Lean and Fat, Grilled, 3oz (85g)	8	3	72	6
Lean and Fat, Raw, 1 lb (453.6g)	40	17	272	30
Lean, Grilled, 3oz (85g)	5	2	71	5
Lean, Raw, 1 lb (453.6g)	18	7	259	20
Rump Steak				
Lean and Fat, Grilled, 3oz (85g)	15	6	77	10
Lean and Fat, Raw, 1 lb (453.6g)	92	39	313	55
Shank Crosscuts				
Lean and Fat, Simmered, 3oz (85g)	10	4	67	7
Lean and Fat, Raw, 1 lb (453.6g)	35	14	195	24
Lean, Simmered, 3oz (85g)	5	2	66	5
Lean, Raw, 1 lb (453.6g)	18	6	177	15
Sirloin				
Lean and Fat, Grilled, 3oz (85g)	15	6	77	10
Lean and Fat, Raw, 1 lb (453.6g)	92	39	313	55
Lean, Grilled, 3oz (85g)	7	3	76	7
Lean, Raw, 1 lb (453.6g)	23	8	277	22
Steaks – *See under individual cuts and also under Steaks*				
Suet				
1oz (28.35g)	27	15	19	16
4oz (113g)	106	59	77	64
Sweetbreads				
Calf, Braised, 3oz (85g)	3	1	396	21
Calf, Raw, 3.5oz (100g)	2	1	250	14
Braised, 3oz (85g)	21	7	250	20
Raw, 4oz (113g)	23	8	252	21
Raw, 1 lb (452g)	92	32	1008	82
T-bone Steak				
Lean and Fat, Grilled, 3oz (85g)	21	9	71	12
Lean and Fat, Raw, 1 lb (453.6g)	119	51	322	67
Lean, Grilled, 3oz (85g)	9	4	68	7
Lean, Raw, 1 lb (453.6g)	36	15	272	28

	TOTAL FAT (g)	SATURATED FAT (g)	CHOLES-TEROL (mg)	CQ
Tenderloin				
Lean and Fat, Grilled, 3oz (85g)	15	6	72	10
Lean and Fat, Roasted, 3oz (85g)	19	8	74	11
Lean and Fat, Raw, 1 lb (453.6g)	82	35	313	51
Lean, Grilled, 3oz (85g)	8	3	71	7
Lean, Roasted, 3oz (85g)	10	4	73	7
Lean, Raw, 1 lb (453.6g)	30	12	281	26
Thymus – *See* Sweetbreads				
Tongue				
Calf, Braised, 1 Slice (20g)	1	1	20	2
Calf, Raw, 3.5oz (100g)	5	3	70	7
Potted or Devilled, 3.5oz (100g)	23	10	110	15
Simmered, 3oz (85g)	18	8	91	12
Smoked, 3.5oz (100g)	29	14	68	18
Whole, Tinned or Pickled, 3.5oz (100g)	20	9	90	13
Raw, 4oz (113g)	18	8	98	13
Raw, 1 lb (452g)	73	31	392	51
Top Loin				
Lean and Fat, Grilled, 3oz (85g)	16	7	67	10
Lean and Fat, Raw, 1 lb (453.6g)	104	45	313	61
Lean, Grilled, 3oz (85g)	8	3	65	6
Lean, Raw, 1 lb (453.6g)	29	12	268	25
Tripe				
Pickled, 3.5oz (100g)	1	1	68	4
Raw, 4oz (113g)	5	2	107	8
Raw, 1 lb (452g)	18	9	428	31
Wedge-bone Sirloin				
Lean and Fat, Grilled, 3oz (85g)	15	6	77	10
Lean and Fat, Raw, 1 lb (453.6g)	92	39	313	55
Lean, Grilled, 3oz (85g)	7	3	76	7
Lean, Raw, 1 lb (453.6g)	23	8	277	22

Beef: Dishes

	TOTAL FAT (g)	SATURATED FAT (g)	CHOLES-TEROL (mg)	CQ
Beef and Vegetable Stew				
Tinned, 15oz Tin (425g)	13	4	60	7
With Lean Chuck, 1 Cup (245g)	11	5	64	8
Beef Broth and Tomato Juice				
Tinned, 5.5 Fl.oz Tin (168g)	0	0	0	0
Beef Bourguignonne				
Home Recipe, 1 Portion	32	13	112	19
Beef Burger				
Grilled, 3oz (85g)	17	7	80	11

	TOTAL FAT (g)	SATURATED FAT (g)	CHOLES-TEROL (mg)	CQ
Beef Pie				
Commercial, Frozen, 3.5oz (100g)	10	3	18	4
Home Recipe, Baked, 1 Piece (⅓ Pie) (210g)	31	8	44	11
Bolognaise Sauce				
With Mince, Home Recipe, 1 Cup	33	9	75	13
Carpaccio (Thin-sliced Beef with Olive Oil Sauce)				
Home Recipe, 1 Portion	15	2	12	3
Chilli con Carne				
With Mince, Home Recipe, 1 Cup	8	3	133	10
Lasagne				
With Mince, Home Recipe, 1 Portion	21	9	79	13
Meatloaf				
Home Recipe, 1 Serving (100g)	13	6	65	9
Moussaka				
With Mince, Home Recipe, 1 Serving (225g)	30	11	90	15
Roast Beef				
Frozen Dinner with Potatoes, Peas and Sweetcorn, 3.5oz (100g)	3	2	50	5
Home Recipe, 1 Portion	26	11	72	14
Tinned, 3.5oz (100g)	13	5	80	9
Roast Beef Sandwich				
1 Sandwich (139g)	14	4	52	6
Shepherd's Pie				
With Mince, Home Recipe, 1 Portion	24	9	77	13
Steak and Kidney Pie				
Home Recipe, 1 Portion	30	22	378	41
Steak au Poivre				
Home Recipe, 1 Portion	41	22	132	29
Stuffed Peppers				
With Minced Beef and Breadcrumb Filling, 1 Pepper (185g)	10	5	70	8

Beef: Prepared Meats

	TOTAL FAT (g)	SATURATED FAT (g)	CHOLES-TEROL (mg)	CQ
Bierwurst				
1 Slice (23g)	7	3	14	4
Bologna				
1 Slice (28.35g)	8	3	16	4
Chipolatas				
Cooked, 3 Sausages	27	13	236	25
Corned Beef				
Jellied Loaf, 2 Slices (56.7g)	4	2	27	3
Tinned, 1 Slice (21g)	3	1	18	2
Tinned, with Potato, 15.5oz Tin (439g)	50	24	145	31
Dried Beef				
1oz (28.35g)	1	1	12	1
Smoked, Creamed, 1 Cup (245g)	25	14	98	19

	TOTAL FAT (g)	SATURATED FAT (g)	CHOLES- TEROL (mg)	CQ
Frankfurter				
1 Frankfurter (57g)	16	7	35	9
Ham and Beef Bologna				
1 Slice (28.35g)	4	2	20	3
Jellied Beef Luncheon Meat				
2 Slices (56.7g)	2	1	19	2
Pastrami				
2 Slices (56.7g)	17	6	53	9
Pickled Tongue				
3.5oz (100g)	20	9	90	13
Pickled Tripe				
3.5oz (100g)	1	1	68	4
Potted Beef				
5½oz Tin (156g)	30	14	122	20
1 Cup (225g)	43	20	176	29
Potted Tongue				
3.5oz (100g)	23	10	110	15
Pressed Beef				
Loaf, 2 Slices (56.7g)	15	6	36	8
Salami				
Smoked, 1 Slice (23g)	5	2	15	3
Sausage				
Grilled, 1 Sausage (68g)	21	7	48	10
Meat, Raw, 1 lb (454g)	107	53	948	101
Smoked, Cooked, 1 Sausage (43g)	12	5	29	6
Smoked Beef				
Dried, Creamed, 1 Cup (245g)	25	14	98	19
Smoked Chopped Beef				
2 Slices (56.7g)	3	1	26	2
Smoked Tongue				
3.5oz (100g)	29	14	68	18
Thin-sliced Beef				
5 Slices (21g)	1	0	9	1
Beer – *See under* Alcohol				
Beetroot				
Boiled, 2 Medium Beetroot (100g)	0	0	0	0
Fresh, 2 Medium Beetroot (163g)	0	0	0	0
Harvard, Tinned, 1 Cup Slices (246g)	0	0	0	0
Pickled, Tinned, 1 Cup Slices (227g)	0	0	0	0
Tinned, 1 Cup (246g)	0	0	0	0
Beetroot Greens				
Boiled, 1 Cup (144g)	0	0	0	0
Fresh, 1 Cup, 1-in Pieces (38g)	0	0	0	0

	TOTAL FAT (g)	SATURATED FAT (g)	CHOLES- TEROL (mg)	CO
Bilberries				
Frozen, 1 Cup Thawed (230g)	0	0	0	0
Fresh, 1 Cup (145g)	1	0	0	0
Tinned, 1 Cup (256g)	1	0	0	0

BISCUITS
See also under Crackers

	TOTAL FAT (g)	SATURATED FAT (g)	CHOLES- TEROL (mg)	CO
Assorted Biscuits				
4 Biscuits (35g)	7	1	14	2
Brownies				
Commercial, with Egg, Water and Nuts, 1 Brownie (20g)	4	1	9	1
Commercial, with Nuts and Chocolate Icing, 1 Brownie (24.5g)	5	2	10	2
Home Recipe, with Nuts and Butter, 1 Brownie (20g)	6	2	22	3
Home Recipe, with Nuts and Vegetable Shortening, 1 Brownie (20g)	6	1	17	2
Butter Biscuits				
Thin, Rich, 4 Biscuits (50g)	9	4	38	6
Cheese Biscuits				
10 Round Biscuits (34.4g)	7	3	11	3
Cheese Sandwich Type				
4 Sandwiches (28g)	7	2	5	2
Chocolate Biscuits				
4 Biscuits (50g)	8	2	19	3
Chocolate Chip				
Commercial, 4 Biscuits (42g)	9	3	16	4
Home Recipe, made with Butter, 4 Biscuits (40g)	11	5	39	7
Home Recipe, made with Vegetable Shortening, 4 Biscuits (40g)	12	3	20	4
Coconut Biscuits				
4 Biscuits (36g)	9	3	39	5
Digestive Biscuits				
Chocolate Coated, 1 Biscuit (13g)	3	1	0	1
Chocolate Coated, 4 Biscuits (50g)	12	4	0	4
Plain, 1 Biscuit (14.2g)	1	0	0	0
Plain, 4 Biscuits (56.8g)	5	1	0	1
Plain, 1 Cup Crumbs (85g)	8	2	0	2
Fig Bars				
4 Biscuits (56g)	3	1	22	2
Ginger Biscuits				
4 Biscuits (28g)	2	1	11	1
Ladyfingers				
4 Ladyfingers (44g)	3	1	157	9

	TOTAL FAT (g)	SATURATED FAT (g)	CHOLES- TEROL (mg)	CQ
Macaroons				
2 Biscuits (38g)	9	6	41	8
Marshmallows				
4 Biscuits covered with Coconut (72g)	10	6	55	9
4 Biscuits covered with Chocolate (52g)	7	4	40	6
Oatmeal				
With Raisins, 4 Biscuits (52g)	8	2	20	3
Peanut Biscuits				
4 Biscuits (50g)	10	2	19	3
Raisin				
4 Biscuits (71g)	4	1	28	2
Rich Tea Biscuits				
4 Biscuits (50g)	12	3	1	3
Sandwich Type Biscuits				
4 Biscuits ($3\frac{1}{8} \times 1\frac{1}{4}$in) (60g)	14	4	23	5
4 Biscuits ($1\frac{3}{4}$in Diam) (40g)	9	2	16	3
Shortbread				
4 Biscuits (30g)	7	2	12	2
Sugar Wafers				
4 Biscuits ($3\frac{1}{2} \times 1 \times \frac{1}{2}$in) (38g)	7	2	15	3
4 Biscuits ($2\frac{1}{2} \times \frac{3}{4} \times \frac{1}{4}$in) (14g)	3	1	5	1
Vanilla Wafers				
4 Regular, $1\frac{3}{4}$in Diameter (16g)	3	1	6	1
Vienna Biscuits				
Home Recipe, made with Butter, 4 Biscuits (32g)	5	3	24	4
Home Recipe, made with Vegetable Shortening, 4 Biscuits (32g)	5	1	12	2
Water Biscuits				
10 Biscuits (28.4g)	3	1	0	1
1 Cup Crumbs (70g)	8	2	0	2
Whole-wheat Biscuits				
3.5oz (100g)	14	3	0	3
Bitter Melon – *See* Balsam-pear				
Blackberries				
Fresh, 1 Cup (144g)	1	0	0	0
Frozen, 1 Cup (151g)	1	0	0	0
Tinned, 1 Cup (256g)	1	0	0	0
Juice, Tinned, 1 Cup (100g)	1	0	0	0
Blancmange				
1 Cup (255g)	10	6	36	7
Borage				
Boiled, 3.5oz (100g)	1	0	0	0
Fresh, 1 Cup, 1-in Pieces (89g)	1	0	0	0

	TOTAL FAT (g)	SATURATED FAT (g)	CHOLES-TEROL (mg)	CQ
Bran				
100% Wheat Bran, 1 Cup (66g)	3	1	0	1
Corn Bran, 1 Cup (36g)	1	0	0	0
Rice Bran, 1 Tbsp (13.6g)	14	3	0	3
Rice Bran, 1 Cup (218g)	218	43	0	43
Brazilnuts				
1oz (6–8 Kernels) (28.4g)	19	5	0	5
1 Cup (32 Kernels) (140g)	93	23	0	23

BREAD

	TOTAL FAT (g)	SATURATED FAT (g)	CHOLES-TEROL (mg)	CQ
Bagels				
Plain, 1 Bagel	1	0	0	0
Breadcrumbs				
Dry, 1 Cup (100g)	5	1	5	1
Breadstuffing Mix				
Dry, 1 Cup Crumbs (70g)	3	1	3	1
Dry, 1 Cup Cubes (30g)	1	0	1	0
With Water, Table Fat and Egg, 1 Cup (200g)	26	13	132	20
With Water and Table Fat, 1 Cup (140g)	31	16	90	21
Crisp Bread				
4 Pieces (28.35g)	3	1	6	1
Croissant				
With Butter, 1 Croissant	25	14	216	25
Crumpet				
With Butter, 1 Crumpet	6	2	13	3
Dough				
Frozen, Unraised, 1 Loaf or 24 Rolls (680g)	34	8	34	10
1 Roll (28g)	1	0	1	0
French or Vienna				
Fresh, 1 Slice (35g)	1	0	1	0
Toasted, 3 Slices (100g)	4	1	4	1
Granary				
1 Slice (25g)	1	0	1	0
Italian				
1 Slice (30g)	0	0	0	0
Pumpernickel				
1 Slice (32g)	0	0	0	0
Raisin				
1 Slice (25g)	1	0	1	0
Raisin Rolls and Buns				
2 Buns (100g)	3	1	3	1
Home Recipe, Made with Milk, 1 Roll (35g)	3	1	12	1
Rolls and Buns				
Commercial, Brown and Serve, 1 Roll (26g)	2	1	2	1
Hard Crust, 1 Roll (25g)	1	0	1	0

	TOTAL FAT (g)	SATURATED FAT (g)	CHOLES- TEROL (mg)	CQ
Soft, 1 Roll (28g)	2	0	2	0
Sweet, 2 Buns (100g)	9	2	9	2
Rusk				
Hard Crisp Bread or Toast, 1 Rusk (9g)	1	0	1	0
13 Rusks (113g)	10	3	10	3
Rye				
Crispbread, Whole-grain, 10 Wafers (65g)	1	0	1	0
8oz Package (227g)	3	0	2	0
Pumpernickel, 1 Slice (32g)	0	0	0	0
Salt-rising				
1 Slice (24g)	1	0	1	0
Sourdough				
1 Slice (24g)	1	0	1	0
Sticks				
Vienna Bread Type, 1 Stick (35g)	1	0	1	0
White Bread				
1 Slice (23g)	1	0	1	0
Whole-wheat Bread				
1 Slice (28g)	1	0	1	0
Breadfruit				
1 Cup (220g)	1	2	0	2

BREAKFAST CEREALS

	TOTAL FAT (g)	SATURATED FAT (g)	CHOLES- TEROL (mg)	CQ
40% Bran Flakes				
1 Cup (39g)	1	0	0	0
100% Wheat Bran				
1 Cup (66g)	3	1	0	1
All-Bran				
1 Cup (35.4g)	1	1	0	1
Bran Buds				
1 Cup (84g)	2	2	0	2
Cheerios				
1 Cup (42.6g)	3	0	0	0
Cocoa Krispies				
1 Cup (36g)	1	0	0	0
Corn Bran				
1 Cup (36g)	1	0	0	0
Corn Flakes				
1 Cup (36g)	0	0	0	0
Honey and Nut, 1 Cup (56g)	3	3	0	3
Cream of Rice				
Cooked with Water, 1 Cup (244g)	0	1	0	0
Cream of Wheat				
Cooked with Water, 1 Cup (241g)	1	1	0	0

	TOTAL FAT (g)	SATURATED FAT (g)	CHOLES-TEROL (mg)	CU
Crispy Rice				
1 Cup (28g)	0	0	0	0
Crispy Wheats 'n Raisins				
1 Cup (43g)	1	1	0	1
Farina				
Cooked with Water, 1 Cup (233g)	0	0	0	0
Frosted Rice Krispies				
1 Cup (28.4g)	0	0	0	0
Grape-Nuts				
1oz (28.4g)	0	1	0	1
1 Cup (113.4g)	0	4	0	4
Grape-Nuts Flakes				
1 Cup (40g)	0	2	0	2
Kellogg's 40% Bran Flakes				
1 Cup (39g)	1	1	0	0
Most				
1 Cup (52g)	1	0	0	0
Muesli				
Homemade, (Oats, Wheat Germ), 1 Cup (122g)	33	6	0	6
Toasted, 1 Cup (113g)	20	13	0	13
Oat Flakes				
Fortified (Oat With Other Grains), 1 Cup (48g)	1	1	0	1
Oats				
Instant, Prepared with Water, 1 Cup (100g)	1	0	0	0
Rolled or Porridge, Dry, 1 Cup (81g)	5	1	0	1
Porridge				
Made with Whole Milk, 1 Cup (220g)	17	9	50	11
Made with Skimmed Milk, 1 Cup (220g)	6	1	6	2
Made with ½ Skimmed Milk, ½ Water, 1 Cup (220g)	5	1	3	1
Made with Water, 1 Cup (234g)	2	0	0	0
Puffed Rice				
1 Cup (14g)	0	0	0	0
Puffed Wheat				
1 Cup (12g)	0	0	0	0
Raisin Bran				
1 Cup (36.9g)	1	2	0	2
Rice Krispies				
1 Cup (28.4g)	0	1	0	1
Shredded Wheat				
Large Biscuit, 2 Biscuits (37.8g)	0	0	0	0
Small Biscuit, 1 Cup (40.8g)	1	0	0	0
Special K				
1 Cup (28.4g)	0	1	0	1
Sugar Frosted Flakes				
1 Cup (35g)	0	2	0	2

	TOTAL FAT (g)	SATURATED FAT (g)	CHOLES- TEROL (mg)	CQ
Sugar Smacks				
1 Cup (28.4g)	1	1	0	1
Sugar-Frosted Wheat Biscuits				
4 Biscuits (31.0g)	0	0	0	0
Team				
1 Cup (42g)	1	2	0	2
Toasted Wheat Germ				
1 Cup (113g)	12	2	0	2
Wheaties				
1 Cup (28.4g)	1	0	0	0
Wheetabix				
2 Biscuits (38g)	1	0	0	0
Broccoli				
Boiled, 1 Cup Chopped (170g)	1	0	0	0
Fresh, 1 Cup Chopped (90g)	0	0	0	0
Brussels Sprouts				
Boiled, 1 Cup (155g)	1	0	0	0
Fresh, 1 Cup (90g)	0	0	0	0
Buckwheat				
Whole-grain, Steamed, 3.5oz (100g)	2	0	0	0
Bulgar Wheat				
Steamed, 1 Cup (175g)	3	0	0	0
Tinned, 1 Cup (135g)	5	1	0	1
Burdock Root				
Boiled, 1 Cup, 1-in Pieces (125g)	0	0	0	0
Fresh, 1 Cup, 1-in Pieces (118g)	0	0	0	0
Burrito				
With Beans, 2 Regular (217g)	14	7	5	7
With Beans and Beef, 2 Regular (231g)	18	8	48	11
With Beans and Cheese, 2 Regular (186g)	12	7	27	8
With Beans, Cheese and Beef, 2 Regular (203g)	13	7	125	13
With Beef, 2 Regular (220g)	21	10	65	14
Butter Oil (Ghee)				
1 Cup (205g)	204	127	525	154
1 Tbsp (12.8g)	13	8	33	10
Butter				
Hard, 1 Pat (5g)	4	3	11	3
4oz (113.4g)	92	57	248	70

	TOTAL FAT (g)	SATURATED FAT (g)	CHOLES-TEROL (mg)	CO
Whipped, 1 Pat (3.8g)	3	2	8	2
4oz (75.6g)	61	38	166	47
Butterbur				
Boiled, 1 Cup (100g)	0	0	0	0
Tinned, 1 Cup (124g)	0	0	0	0
Fresh, 1 Cup (94g)	0	0	0	0
Cabbage				
Chinese, Boiled, 1 Cup Shredded (170g)	0	0	0	0
Chinese, Fresh, 1 Cup Shredded (70g)	0	0	0	0
Red, Boiled, 1 Cup Shredded (75g)	0	0	0	0
Red, Fresh, 1 Cup Shredded (70g)	0	0	0	0
Savoy, Boiled, 1 Cup Shredded (145g)	0	0	0	0
Savoy, Fresh, 1 Cup Shredded (70g)	0	0	0	0
Spring, Fresh				
1 Cup Shredded (70g)	0	0	0	0
1 Head (908g)	2	0	0	0
White, Boiled				
1 Cup Shredded (150g)	0	0	0	0
1 Head (1262g)	3	0	0	0
White, Fresh				
1 Cup Shredded (70g)	0	0	0	0
1 Head (908g)	2	0	0	0

CAKES
See also Icing

	TOTAL FAT (g)	SATURATED FAT (g)	CHOLES-TEROL (mg)	CO
Angelfood				
Made from Mix with Water, 1 Portion (80g)	0	0	0	0
Home Recipe, 1 Portion (90g)	0	0	0	0
Brownies				
Home Recipe, with Nuts and Butter, 1 Brownie (20g)	6	2	22	3
Home Recipe, with Nuts and Vegetable Shortening, 1 Brownie (20g)	6	1	17	2
Caramel Cake				
Cake and Icing made with Butter, 1 Portion (158g)	21	11	147	19
Cake made with Vegetable Shortening, Icing made with Butter 1 Portion (158g)	23	7	102	12
Uniced, Cake made with Butter, 1 Portion (108g)	17	9	124	15
Uniced, Cake made with Vegetable Shortening, 1 Portion (108g)	19	5	84	9

	TOTAL FAT (g)	SATURATED FAT (g)	CHOLES- TEROL (mg)	CO
Chocolate Cake				
Cake and Choc-Icing made with Butter, 1 Small Cake (44g)	7	4	29	5
Cake made with Vegetable Shortening, Choc-Icing made with Butter, 1 Small Cake (44g)	7	3	21	4
Cake and White Icing made with Butter, 1 Small Cake (44g)	6	3	30	5
Cake made with Vegetable Shortening, White Icing made with Butter 1 Small Cake (44g)	6	2	21	4
Malt, Cake made with Eggs, Icing made with Butter 1 Portion (132g)	12	4	72	8
Cottage Pudding				
Made with Butter, No Sauce, 1 Portion (73g)	8	4	59	7
Made with Butter, with Sauce, 1 Portion (99g)	8	4	58	7
Made with Vegetable Shortening, No Sauce, 1 Portion (73g)	8	2	44	5
Made with Vegetable Shortening, with Sauce 1 Portion with Sauce (99g)	9	3	44	5
Fruitcake				
Light, made with Butter, 1 Portion (43g)	7	2	11	3
Light, made with Vegetable Shortening, 1 Portion (43g)	7	2	3	2
Rich, made with Butter, 1 Portion (43g)	6	2	28	3
Rich, made with Vegetable Shortening, 1 Portion (43g)	7	1	19	2
Genoa				
Made with Butter, 1 Portion (85g)	10	5	68	9
Made with Vegetable Shortening, 1 Portion (85g)	11	3	46	5
Gingerbread				
Baked from Mix, 1 Portion (71g)	5	1	1	1
Made with Butter, 1 Portion (132g)	13	7	87	11
Made with Vegetable Shortening, 1 Portion (132g)	14	4	57	6
Honey Spice Cake				
Made with Eggs, Caramel icing made with Butter 1 Portion (154g)	17	5	90	9
Madeira Cake				
Made with Butter, 1 Portion (83g)	12	7	33	8
Made with Vegetable Shortening, 1 Portion (83g)	13	4	2	4
Marble Cake				
Made with Eggs, with Boiled White Icing, 1 Portion (131g)	11	3	67	7
Mocha Cake				
Made with Eggs and Milk, 1 Portion (54g)	5	1	33	3

	TOTAL FAT (g)	SATURATED FAT (g)	CHOLES- TEROL (mg)	CQ
Plain Cake				
Cake and Icing made with Butter, 1 Portion (123g)	15	8	42	10
Made with Butter, with Coconut icing, 1 Portion (122g)	15	9	33	11
Made with Egg Whites, Choc-Icing made with Butter 1 Portion (143g)	15	6	3	6
Made with Vegetable Shortening, Icing made with Butter 1 Portion (123g)	16	5	10	5
Made with Vegetable Shortening with Coconut icing, 1 Portion (122g)	16	6	2	6
Pound Cake				
Made with Butter, 1 Portion (62g)	11	5	118	11
Made with Vegetable Shortening, 1 Portion (62g)	12	3	95	8
Rock Cakes				
1 Cake (55g)	9	3	22	4
Sponge Cake				
1 Portion (65g)	4	1	161	9
Layered with Cream, made with Butter, 1 Portion (103g)	9	4	104	10
Layered with Cream, made with Vegetable Shortening 1 Portion (103g)	10	3	89	7
Vanilla Cake				
Cake and Choc-Icing made with Butter, 1 Portion (139g)	18	10	97	15
Cake and Icing made with Butter, 1 Portion (137g)	15	8	99	13
Cake made with Butter, No Icing, 1 Portion (97g)	12	6	90	11
Made with Vegetable Shortening, Choc-icing made with Butter, 1 Portion (139g)	19	7	69	11
Made with Vegetable Shortening, White Icing made with Butter 1 Portion (137g)	16	5	71	9
Made with Vegetable Shortening, 1 Portion (97g)	14	4	63	7
Calabash				
White-flowered Gourd, Boiled, 1 Cup, 1-in Cubes (146g)	0	0	0	0
Cape-gooseberries				
Fresh, 1 Cup (140g)	1	0	0	0
Carambola				
Fresh, 1 Fruit (127g)	0	0	0	0

CARBONATED DRINKS

	TOTAL FAT (g)	SATURATED FAT (g)	CHOLES- TEROL (mg)	CO
Club Soda				
12 Fl.oz Tin (355g)	0	0	0	0
Cola				
12 Fl.oz Tin (370g)	0	0	0	0
Cream Soda				
12 Fl.oz Tin (371g)	0	0	0	0
Ginger Ale				
12 Fl.oz Tin (366g)	0	0	0	0
Lemonade				
12 Fl.oz Tin (368g)	0	0	0	0
Lemon-lime Soda				
12 Fl.oz Tin (368g)	0	0	0	0
Low Calorie Cola				
12 Fl.oz Tin (355g)	0	0	0	0
Low Calorie Drinks				
12 Fl.oz Tin (355g)	0	0	0	0
Orange				
12 Fl.oz Tin (372g)	0	0	0	0
Root Beer				
12 Fl.oz Tin (370g)	0	0	0	0
Tonic Water				
12 Fl.oz (366g)	0	0	0	0
Cardoon				
Boiled, 3.5oz (100g)	0	0	0	0
Fresh, 1 Cup Shredded (178g)	0	0	0	0
Carissa				
Fresh, 1 Fruit (20g)	0	0	0	0
Carrot Juice				
1 Cup (224g)	0	0	0	0
Carrots				
Boiled, 1 Cup Slices (150g)	0	0	0	0
Fresh, 1 Cup Shredded (110g)	0	0	0	0
Tinned, 1 Cup Slices (200g)	1	0	0	0
Cashew Nuts				
Dry Roasted, 1 Cup (137g)	64	13	0	13
Cassava				
3.5oz (100g)	0	0	0	0
Cauliflower				
Boiled, 1 Cup, 1-in Pieces (125g)	0	0	0	0
Fresh, 1 Cup, 1-in Pieces (120g)	0	0	0	0

	TOTAL FAT (g)	SATURATED FAT (g)	CHOLES- TEROL (mg)	CQ
Cauliflower Cheese				
1 Portion (225g)	18	10	38	12
Celeriac				
Boiled, 3.5oz (100g)	0	0	0	0
Fresh, 1 Cup (156g)	1	0	0	0
Celery				
Boiled, 1 Cup Diced (150g)	0	0	0	0
Fresh, 1 Cup Diced (120g)	0	0	0	0
CEREALS AND GRAIN				
100% Wheat Bran, 1 Cup (66g)	3	1	0	1
Corn Bran, 1 Cup (36g)	1	0	0	0
Oats, Regular Dry				
1 serving (27g)	2	0	0	0
1 Cup (81g)	5	1	0	1
Toasted Wheat Germ				
1oz (28.4g)	3	1	0	1
1 Cup (113g)	12	2	0	2
Whole Wheat				
Cooked with Water, 1 Cup (242g)	1	1	0	0
Dry, 1 Cup (94g)	2	0	0	0
$\frac{1}{3}$ Cup (31gm)	1	0	0	0
Chard, Swiss				
Boiled, 1 Cup Chopped (175g)	0	0	0	0
Fresh, 1 Cup Chopped (48g)	0	0	0	0
Charlotte Russe, with Lady Fingers, Whipped Cream Filling				
1 Serving (114g)	17	8	225	20
Chayote – *See* Custard Marrow				
CHEESE				
Blue				
1oz (28g)	8	5	21	6
Brie				
1oz (28g)	8	5	28	6
Camembert				
1oz (28g)	7	4	20	5
Caraway				
1oz (28g)	8	5	26	7
Cheddar				
1oz (28g)	9	6	29	7
1 Cup, Shredded (113g)	37	24	119	30

	TOTAL FAT (g)	SATURATED FAT (g)	CHOLES- TEROL (mg)	CO
Cheshire				
1oz (28g)	9	6	29	7
Cottage				
Creamed, 1 Cup (210g)	10	6	31	8
Creamed, with Fruit, 1 Cup (226g)	8	5	25	6
Low-fat, 1% Fat, 1 Cup (226g)	2	2	10	2
Low-fat, 2% Fat, 1 Cup (226g)	4	3	19	4
Cream Cheese				
1oz (28g)	10	6	31	8
Curd Cheese				
Uncreamed, Dry, 1 Cup (145g)	1	0	10	1
Edam				
1oz (28g)	8	5	25	6
Emmental				
1oz (28g)	8	5	26	6
Feta				
1oz (28g)	6	4	25	5
Fontina				
1oz (28g)	9	5	33	7
Gjetost				
1oz (28g)	8	5	26	7
Gouda				
1oz (28g)	8	5	32	7
Gruyère				
1oz (28g)	9	5	31	7
Limburger				
1oz (28g)	8	5	25	6
Mozzarella				
Part Skimmed Milk, 1oz (28g)	5	3	16	4
Whole Milk, 1oz (28g)	6	4	22	5
Muenster				
1oz (28g)	8	5	27	7
Neufchâtel				
1oz (28g)	7	4	21	5
Parmesan				
Grated, 1 Tbsp (5g)	2	1	4	1
1oz (28g)	8	5	22	6
Processed Cheese				
Pasteurized, 1oz (28g)	9	6	26	7
Pasteurized, Swiss, 1oz (28g)	7	5	24	6
Port de Salut				
1oz (28g)	8	5	34	6
Provolone				
1oz (28g)	8	5	19	6
Ricotta				
Part Skimmed Milk, 1 Cup (246g)	20	12	76	16
Whole Milk, 1 Cup (246g)	32	20	125	27

	TOTAL FAT (g)	SATURATED FAT (g)	CHOLES- TEROL (mg)	CQ
Romano				
1oz (28g)	8	5	29	6
Roquefort				
1oz (28g)	9	5	25	7
Swiss				
1oz (28g)	8	5	26	6
Tilsit				
Whole Milk, 1oz (28g)	7	5	29	6
Cheese and Tomato Sandwich				
1 Sandwich (100g)	25	15	71	19
Cheeseburger				
1 Regular	16	7	41	9
1 Double-decker	28	13	110	19
Cheeseburger with Ham or Bacon and Condiments				
1 Burger with Ham	48	21	122	27
1 Burger with Bacon	37	16	112	22
Cheese Cake				
With Fruit Topping, 1 Portion (⅙ of Cake)	21	12	55	15
Cheese Fondue				
3.5oz (100g)	18	9	224	20
Cheese Pudding				
1 Serving (140g)	15	8	182	17
Cheese Sauce				
Prepared with Milk, 1 Cup (279.2g)	17	9	53	12
Cheese Soufflé				
1 Portion (110g)	19	10	204	20
Cheese Spread				
Pasteurized Processed, 1oz (28g)	6	4	16	5
Cheese Straws				
Made with Lard, 10 Pieces (60g)	18	8	32	10
Made with Vegetable Shortening, 10 Pieces (60g)	18	6	19	7
Cherries				
Acerola, Juice, 1 Cup (242g)	1	0	0	0
Fresh				
10 Fruits (68g)	1	0	0	0
1 Cup (145g)	1	0	0	0
Frozen, Thawed, 1 Cup (259g)	0	0	0	0

	TOTAL FAT (g)	SATURATED FAT (g)	CHOLES-TEROL (mg)	CO
Maraschino, Bottled, 3.5oz (100g)	0	0	0	0
Tinned, 1 Cup (244g)	0	0	0	0
Chervil				
Fresh, 3.5oz (100g)	1	0	0	0
Chewing Gum				
1 Piece (1.7g)	0	0	0	0

CHICKEN

Capons (whole birds)
Meat and Skin and Giblets and Neck

Roasted, 1 Chicken (1418g)	166	47	1461	120
Whole Bird				
Raw, 1 Chicken (2152g)	364	105	1872	200
Meat and Skin				
Roasted, 1 Portion (196g)	23	6	169	15
½ Chicken (637g)	74	21	548	48
Raw, 1 Portion (297g)	51	15	223	26
½ Chicken (964g)	165	48	723	84
Giblets				
Simmered, 1 Cup (145g)	8	3	629	34
Raw (115g)	6	2	336	19

Dishes
Chicken and Noodles

1 Cup (240g)	19	6	96	11
Chicken Casserole				
1 Cup (245g)	34	13	186	22
Chicken Chow Mein				
Without Noodles, Home Recipe, 1 Cup (250g)	10	2	78	6
Chicken Dinner				
Frozen Fried Chicken and Mixed Vegetables, 1 Serving (100g)	9	3	49	5
Chicken Fricassee				
1 Cup (240g)	22	7	96	12
Chicken Liver Pâté, Tinned				
1 Tbsp (13g)	2	1	51	3
1oz (28.35g)	4	1	111	7
Chicken Pie				
Baked, Home Recipe, 1 Piece (232g)	31	11	72	15
Commercial, 1 Piece (100g)	12	3	13	4
Chicken Roll				
Light Meat, 2 Slices (56.7g)	4	1	28	3

	TOTAL FAT (g)	SATURATED FAT (g)	CHOLESTEROL (mg)	CO
Chicken Salad				
1 Portion (218g)	2	1	72	4
Chicken Salad Sandwich Spread				
1oz (28.35g)	4	1	9	1
Chicken Sandwich				
Plain, 1 Sandwich (182g)	29	9	60	12
With Cheese, 1 Sandwich (228g)	39	12	76	16
Chicken Spread				
Tinned, 1oz (28.35g)	3	1	15	2
Chicken Vegetable Soup				
Tinned, Ready-to-serve, 1 Cup (8 Fl.oz) (240g)	5	1	17	2
1 Tin (19oz) (539g)	11	3	38	5
Fried Chicken				
Breast or Wing, 2 Pieces (163g)	30	8	149	15
Drumstick or Thigh, 2 Pieces (148g)	27	7	165	15
Dinner, Frozen with Mixed Vegetables, 1 Serving (100g)	9	3	49	5
Potted Chicken				
5½oz Tin (156g)	30	14	122	20
1 Cup (225g)	43	20	176	29
Roast Chicken				
1 Portion (210g)	28	8	160	16
1 Chicken (1072g)	140	39	1008	90
Roast Stuffing Mix				
With Water, Table Fat and Egg, 1 Cup (200g)	26	13	132	20
With Water and Table Fat, 1 Cup (140g)	31	16	90	21
Sweet and Sour Chicken				
1 Portion (130g)	18	6	61	9
Tinned Chicken with Broth				
1 Tin, 5oz (142g)	11	3	88	8

Fryers and Broilers
WHOLE BIRDS

	TOTAL FAT (g)	SATURATED FAT (g)	CHOLESTEROL (mg)	CO
Meat, Skin, Giblets and Neck				
Fried, Floured, 1 Portion (212g)	32	9	237	21
1 Chicken (708g)	108	30	793	69
Fried, in Batter, 1 Portion (308g)	54	14	317	30
1 Chicken (1028g)	180	48	1059	101
Roasted, 1 Portion (205g)	27	8	219	19
1 Chicken (682g)	91	25	730	62
Stewed, 1 Portion (225g)	28	8	218	19
1 Chicken (751g)	93	26	729	63
Raw, 1 Chicken (1046g)	155	44	941	92
Meat and Skin				
Fried, Floured, 1 Portion (188g)	28	8	169	16
½ Chicken (314g)	47	13	283	27

	TOTAL FAT (g)	SATURATED FAT (g)	CHOLES-TEROL (mg)	CQ
Fried, in Batter, 1 Portion (280g)	49	13	244	25
½ Chicken (466g)	81	22	405	42
Roasted, 1 Portion (178g)	24	7	157	15
½ Chicken (299g)	41	11	263	25
Stewed, 1 Portion (200g)	25	7	156	15
½ Chicken (334g)	42	12	261	25
Raw, 1 Portion (276g)	42	12	207	22
½ Chicken (460g)	69	20	345	37
Meat Only				
Fried, 1 Portion (140g)	13	3	132	10
Roasted, 1 Portion (140g)	10	3	125	9
Stewed, 1 Portion (140g)	9	3	116	8
Raw, 1 Portion (197g)	6	2	138	8
½ Chicken (329g)	10	3	230	14
Dark Meat and Skin				
Fried, Floured, 1 Portion (110g)	19	5	101	10
½ Chicken (184g)	31	8	169	17
Fried, in Batter, 1 Portion (167g)	31	8	149	16
½ Chicken (278g)	52	14	247	26
Roasted, 1 Portion (101g)	16	4	92	9
½ Chicken (167g)	26	7	152	15
Stewed, 1 Portion (110g)	16	5	90	9
½ Chicken (184g)	27	8	151	15
Raw, 1 Portion (160g)	29	8	130	15
½ Chicken (266g)	49	14	216	25
Dark Meat Only				
Fried, 1 Portion (140g)	16	4	134	11
Roasted, 1 Portion (140g)	14	4	130	10
Stewed, 1 Portion (140g)	13	3	123	10
Raw, 1 Portion (109g)	5	1	87	6
½ Chicken (182g)	8	2	146	9
Light Meat and Skin				
Fried, Floured, 1 Portion (78g)	9	3	68	6
½ Chicken (130g)	16	4	113	10
Fried, in Batter, 1 Portion (113g)	17	5	95	9
½ Chicken (188g)	29	8	158	16
Roasted, 1 Portion (79g)	9	2	66	6
½ Chicken (132g)	14	4	111	10
Stewed, 1 Portion (90g)	9	3	67	6
½ Chicken (150g)	15	4	111	10
Raw, 1 Portion (116g)	13	4	78	8
½ Chicken (194g)	22	6	130	13
Light Meat Only				
Fried, 1 Portion (64g)	4	1	58	4
Roasted, 1 Portion (64g)	3	1	54	4
Stewed, 1 Portion (71g)	3	1	55	4
Raw, 1 Portion (88g)	2	0	51	3
½ Chicken (147g)	2	1	85	5

	TOTAL FAT (g)	SATURATED FAT (g)	CHOLES- TEROL (mg)	CO
PART BIRDS				
Back				
Meat and Skin				
Fried, Floured, 1 Portion (72g)	15	4	64	7
Fried, in Batter, 1 Portion (120g)	26	7	106	12
Roasted, 1 Portion (53g)	11	3	47	5
Stewed, 1 Portion (61g)	11	3	48	5
Raw, ½ Back (99g)	29	8	78	12
Meat Only				
Fried, 1 Portion (58g)	9	2	54	5
Roasted, 1 Portion (40g)	5	1	36	3
Stewed, 1 Portion (42g)	5	1	36	3
Raw, ½ Back (51g)	3	1	41	3
Breast				
Meat and Skin				
Fried, Floured, 1 Portion (98g)	9	2	87	7
Fried, in Batter, 1 Portion (140g)	19	5	119	11
Roasted, 1 Portion (98g)	8	2	82	6
Stewed, 1 Portion (110g)	8	2	83	6
Raw, ½ Breast (145g)	13	4	93	9
Meat Only				
Fried, 1 Portion (86g)	4	1	78	5
Roasted, 1 Portion (86g)	3	1	73	5
Stewed, 1 Portion (95g)	3	1	73	4
Raw, ½ Breast (118g)	2	0	68	4
Drumstick				
Meat and Skin				
Fried, in Batter, 1 Drumstick (72g)	11	3	62	6
Roasted, 1 Drumstick (52g)	6	2	47	4
Stewed, 1 Drumstick (57g)	6	2	47	4
Raw, 1 Drumstick (73g)	6	2	59	5
Meat Only				
Fried, 1 Drumstick (42g)	3	1	40	3
Roasted, 1 Drumstick (44g)	3	1	41	3
Stewed, 1 Drumstick (46g)	3	1	41	3
Fat				
From 1 lb Ready-to-Cook Chicken	22	7	19	7
From ½ Chicken	35	11	30	12
Giblets				
Fried, 1 Cup (145g)	20	6	647	38
Simmered, 1 Cup (145g)	7	2	570	31
Raw (75g)	3	1	197	11
Gizzard				
Simmered, 1 Cup (145g)	5	2	281	16
Raw, 1 Gizzard (37g)	2	0	48	3

	TOTAL FAT (g)	SATURATED FAT (g)	CHOLES-TEROL (mg)	CQ
Heart				
Simmered, 1 Cup (145g)	12	3	351	21
Raw, 1 Heart (6.1g)	1	0	8	1
Leg				
Meat and Skin				
Fried, Floured, 1 Leg (112g)	16	4	105	10
Fried, in Batter, 1 Leg (158g)	26	7	142	14
Roasted, 1 Leg (114g)	15	4	105	10
Stewed, 1 Leg (125g)	16	5	105	10
Raw, 1 Leg (167g)	20	6	139	13
Meat Only				
Fried, 1 Leg (94g)	9	2	93	7
Roasted, 1 Leg (95g)	8	2	89	7
Stewed, 1 Leg (101g)	8	2	90	7
Raw, 1 Leg (130g)	5	1	104	6
Liver				
Simmered, 1 Cup (140g)	8	3	883	47
Raw, 1 Liver (32g)	1	0	141	7
Neck				
Meat and Skin				
Fried, Floured, 1 Neck (36g)	9	2	34	4
Fried, in Batter, 1 Neck (52g)	12	3	47	6
Simmered, 1 Neck (38g)	7	2	27	3
Raw, 1 Neck (50g)	13	4	50	6
Meat Only				
Fried, 1 Neck (22g)	3	1	23	2
Simmered, 1 Neck (18g)	2	0	14	1
Raw, 1 Neck (20g)	2	1	17	1
Skin				
Fried, Floured, from ½ Chicken (56g)	24	7	41	9
Fried, in Batter, from ½ Chicken (190g)	55	15	141	22
Roasted, from ½ Chicken (56g)	23	6	47	9
Stewed, from ½ Chicken (72g)	24	7	45	9
Raw, from ½ Chicken (79g)	26	7	86	12
Thigh				
Meat and Skin				
Fried, Floured, 1 Thigh (62g)	9	3	60	6
Fried, in Batter, 1 Thigh (86g)	14	4	80	8
Roasted, 1 Thigh (62g)	10	3	58	6
Stewed, 1 Thigh (68g)	10	3	57	6
Raw, 1 Thigh (94g)	14	4	79	8

	TOTAL FAT (g)	SATURATED FAT (g)	CHOLES- TEROL (mg)	CQ
Meat Only				
Fried, 1 Thigh (52g)	5	1	53	4
Roasted, 1 Thigh (52g)	6	2	49	4
Stewed, 1 Thigh (55g)	5	2	50	4
Raw, 1 Thigh (69g)	3	1	57	4
Wing				
Meat and Skin				
Fried, Floured, 1 Wing (32g)	7	2	26	3
Fried, in Batter, 1 Wing (49g)	11	3	39	5
Roasted, 1 Wing (34g)	7	2	29	3
Stewed, 1 Wing (40g)	7	2	28	3
Raw, 1 Wing (49g)	8	2	38	4
Meat Only				
Fried, 1 Wing (20g)	2	1	17	1
Roasted, 1 Wing (21g)	2	1	18	1
Stewed, 1 Wing (24g)	2	1	18	1
Raw, 1 Wing (29g)	1	0	17	1
Roasters				
WHOLE BIRDS				
Meat, Skin, Giblets and Neck				
Roasted, 1 Portion (235g)	31	9	221	20
1 Chicken (1072g)	140	39	1008	90
Raw, 1 Chicken (1509g)	233	67	1298	132
Meat and Skin				
Roasted, 1 Portion (210g)	28	8	160	16
½ Chicken (480g)	64	18	365	36
Raw, ½ Chicken (668g)	106	30	488	55
Meat Only				
Roasted, 1 Portion (140g)	9	3	105	8
Raw, ½ Chicken (477g)	13	3	310	19
Dark Meat				
Roasted, 1 Portion (140g)	12	3	105	9
Raw, ½ Chicken (258g)	9	2	186	12
Light Meat				
Roasted, 1 Portion (140g)	6	2	105	7
Raw, ½ Chicken (220g)	4	1	125	7
Giblets				
Simmered, 1 Cup (145g)	8	2	518	28
Raw, Giblets (113g)	6	2	267	15
Stewing				
WHOLE BIRDS				
Meat, Skin and Giblets				
Stewed, 1 Portion (202g)	36	10	206	20
1 Chicken (593g)	107	29	605	60

	TOTAL FAT (g)	SATURATED FAT (g)	CHOLES- TEROL (mg)	CQ
Meat, Skin, Giblets and Neck				
Raw, 1 Chicken (905g)	177	50	787	89
Meat and Skin				
Stewed, 1 Portion (178g)	34	9	141	16
Raw, ½ Chicken (398g)	81	23	283	37
Meat Only				
Stewed, 1 Portion (140g)	17	4	116	10
Raw, ½ Chicken (284g)	18	5	179	13
Dark Meat				
Stewed, 1 Portion (73g)	11	3	69	6
Raw, ½ Chicken (154g)	13	3	119	9
Light Meat				
Stewed, 1 Portion (64g)	5	1	45	4
Raw, ½ Chicken (130g)	6	1	61	4
Giblets				
Simmered, 1 Cup (145g)	14	4	515	30
Raw, Giblets (81g)	8	2	194	12
Chicory, Fresh				
1 Head (53g)	0	0	0	0
Chilli				
See also under Peppers, Sauces				
Chilli con Carne, Home Recipe, 1 Cup	8	3	133	10
Tinned, With Beans, 1 Cup (255g)	14	6	43	8
Chilli Sauce, Red, Tinned, 1 Cup (245g)	2	0	0	0
Chinese Cabbage				
Boiled, 1 Cup Shredded (170g)	0	0	0	0
Fresh, 1 Cup Shredded (70g)	0	0	0	0
Chips				
See also under Potatoes				
Fried in Animal Fat, 1 Regular Portion (76g)	12	6	13	6
1 Large Portion (115g)	19	9	20	10
Fried in Animal Fat and Vegetable Oil, 1 Regular				
Portion (76g)	12	5	11	6
1 Large Portion (115g)	19	8	16	9
Fried in Vegetable Oil, 1 Regular Portion (76g)	12	4	0	4
1 Large Portion (115g)	19	6	0	6
Chives				
Fresh, 1 Tbsp Chopped (3g)	0	0	0	0

	TOTAL FAT (g)	SATURATED FAT (g)	CHOLES-TEROL (mg)	CQ
CHOCOLATE				
See also under Sweets				
Baking Chocolate				
1oz (28g)	15	8	0	8
1 Cup, Grated (132g)	70	39	0	40
Hot Chocolate				
Made with 1 Cup Milk and 2–3 Heaped Teaspoons				
Powder (266g)	9	6	32	7
Chocolate Bar				
Bitter, 3.5oz (100g)	40	22	0	22
Milk, Plain, 3.5oz (100g)	32	18	20	19
Milk, with Almonds, 3.5oz (100g)	36	16	17	17
Milk, with Peanuts, 3.5oz (100g)	38	16	13	17
Semisweet, 3.5oz (100g)	35	20	0	20
Sweet, 3.5oz (100g)	35	20	1	20
With Coconut Centre, 3.5oz (100g)	18	10	1	10
With Fudge, Peanuts and Caramel Centre, 3.5oz (100g)	23	6	2	6
With Nougat and Caramel Centre, 3.5oz (100g)	14	4	5	5
Chocolate Fudge				
Plain, 1oz (28g)	3	1	0	1
With Nuts, 1oz (28g)	5	1	0	1
Chocolate Mints				
1 Mint (35g)	4	1	0	1
Chocolate Shake				
1 Medium (283g)	11	7	37	8
Chocolate Syrup				
1 Tbsp (18.8g)	0	0	0	0
1 Cup (300g)	4	2	0	2
Fudge Type, 2 Tbsp (37.5g)	5	3	0	3
1 Cup (300g)	41	23	0	23
Prepared with 1 Cup Milk and 1 Tbsp Syrup (263g)	8	5	34	7
Chop Suey with Meat				
Home Recipe, 1 Cup (250g)	17	9	100	14
Tinned, 3.5oz (100g)	3	1	12	2
Chow Mein				
Chicken, without Noodles, Home Recipe, 1 Cup (250g)	10	2	78	6
Tinned, 1 Cup (250g)	0	0	8	0
Christmas Pudding				
1 Serving (170g)	81	9	102	14

	TOTAL FAT (g)	SATURATED FAT (g)	CHOLES-TEROL (mg)	CQ
Citron Peel				
Candied, 1oz (28g)	0	0	0	0
Citrus Fruit Drink				
1 Cup (248g)	0	0	0	0
Cocktails – *See under* Alcohol				
Cocoa				
Made with 1 Cup Milk and 2–3 Heaped Teaspoons Powder (266g)	9	6	32	7
Powder, 1oz Packet (3–4 Heaped Tsp) (28.4g)	1	1	1	1
Powder, made with 6 Fl.oz Water and 3–4 Heaped Tsp (206g)	1	1	2	1
Coconut				
Cream, Fresh (Liquid Expressed from Grated Meat), 1 Tbsp (15g)	5	5	0	5
1 Cup (240g)	83	74	0	75
Cream, Tinned (Liquid Expressed from Grated Meat), 1 Tbsp (19g)	3	3	0	3
1 Cup (296g)	53	47	0	47
Meat, Dried (Desiccated), 1oz (28.4g)	18	16	0	16
3.5oz (100g)	65	57	0	58
Meat, Dried (Desiccated), Creamed, 1oz (28.4g)	20	17	0	18
3.5oz (100g)	69	61	0	62
Meat, Dried (Desiccated), Flaked, 1oz (28.4g)	9	8	0	8
1 Cup (77g)	24	22	0	22
Meat, Dried (Desiccated), Shredded, 1oz (28.4g)	10	9	0	9
1 Cup (93g)	33	29	0	30
Meat, Dried (Desiccated), Toasted, 1oz (28.4g)	13	12	0	12
3.5oz (100g)	47	42	0	42
Meat, Fresh, 1 Piece (45g)	15	13	0	13
1 Cup Grated (80g)	27	24	0	24
Milk, Fresh, 1 Cup (240g)	57	51	0	51
Milk, Frozen (Liquid Expressed from Grated Meat and Water) 1 Cup (240g)	50	44	0	45
Milk, Tinned, 1 Cup (226g)	48	43	0	43
Water (Liquid from Coconuts), 1 Cup (240g)	1	0	0	0
Coffee				
Brewed, 6 Fl.oz (177g)	0	0	0	0
Instant, 1 Rounded Tsp Powder (1.8g)	0	0	0	0
6 Fl.oz Water and 1 Rounded Tsp Powder (179g)	0	0	0	0

	TOTAL FAT (g)	SATURATED FAT (g)	CHOLES-TEROL (mg)	CQ
Instant, Cappuccino Flavour, 2 Rounded Tsp Powder (14.2g)	2	2	0	2
6 Fl.oz Water and 2 Rounded Tsp Powder (192g)	2	2	0	2
Instant, French Flavour, 2 Rounded Tsp Powder (11.5g)	3	3	0	3
6 Fl.oz Water and 2 Rounded Tsp Powder (189g)	3	3	0	3
Instant, Mocha Flavour, 2 Rounded Tsp Powder (11.5g)	2	2	0	2
6 Fl.oz Water and 2 Rounded Tsp Powder (188g)	2	2	0	2
Coffee Substitute				
Powder, 1 Tsp (2.3g)	0	0	0	0
6 Fl.oz Water and 1 Tsp Powder	0	0	0	0
Prepared with 6 Fl.oz Milk and 1 Tsp Powder (185g)	6	4	24	5
Cola				
12 Fl.oz Tin (370g)	0	0	0	0
Coleslaw				
1 Cup (138g)	15	2	7	2
Collards				
Boiled, 1 Cup Chopped (170g)	0	0	0	0
Fresh, 1 Cup Chopped (186g)	0	0	0	0
Coriander				
Fresh, ¼ Cup (4g)	0	0	0	0
Corn – See under Sweetcorn				
Corn Flakes				
1 Bowl with Milk	9	5	33	7
Corn Fritters				
1 Fritter (35g)	8	2	31	4
Corn on the Cob				
With Butter, 1 Ear (146g)	3	2	6	2
Cornbread				
Home Recipe, made with Lard, 1 Piece (93g)	6	2	69	5
Home Recipe, made with Vegetable Shortening, 1 Piece (93g)	6	1	65	5

	TOTAL FAT (g)	SATURATED FAT (g)	CHOLES-TEROL (mg)	CQ
Mix, made with Egg and Milk, 1 Piece (100g)	8	3	69	6
Cornflour				
1 Tbsp (8g)	0	0	0	0
Cornmeal				
Whole Ground, Cooked, 1 Cup (122g)	5	1	0	1
Cornsalad				
Fresh, 1 Cup (56g)	0	0	0	0
Courgette				
Boiled, 1 Cup (223g)	0	0	0	0
Fresh, 1 Cup Slices (130g)	0	0	0	0
In Tomato Sauce, Tinned, 1 Cup (227g)	0	0	0	0
Crab				
See also under Fish/Shellfish				
Devilled, 1 Cup (240g)	23	7	245	19
Dressed, 1 Cup (220g)	17	9	308	24
Crab Apples				
Fresh, 1 Cup Slices (110g)	0	0	0	0
Crackers				
Animal, 2oz Package (approximately 22) (57g)	5	1	0	1
10 Crackers (26g)	2	1	0	1
Cheese, 10 Round Crackers (34.4g)	7	3	11	3
10 Cocktail Crackers (10.8g)	2	1	4	1
Cheese Sandwich Type, 1 Packet (6 Sandwiches) (42g)	10	3	7	3
1 Packet (4 Sandwiches) (28g)	7	2	5	2
Cream, 10 Large Crackers (50.4g)	7	2	0	2
10 Small Crackers (28.4g)	4	1	0	1
Matzos, 10 Crackers (38g)	7	2	0	2
Water Biscuits, 10 Crackers (28.4g)	3	1	0	1
1 Cup Crumbs (70g)	8	2	0	2
Whole-wheat, 3.5oz (100g)	14	3	0	3
Cranberries				
Fresh, 1 Cup (110g)	0	0	0	0
Cranberry Juice				
Bottled, 1 Cup (253g)	0	0	0	0
Cranberry Sauce				
Tinned, 1 Cup (277g)	0	0	0	0

	TOTAL FAT (g)	SATURATED FAT (g)	CHOLES- TEROL (mg)	CQ
Cranberry-orange Relish				
Tinned, 1 Cup (275g)	0	0	0	0
Cream				
Coffee or Table, 1 Tbsp (15g)	3	2	10	2
1 Cup (240g)	46	29	159	37
Double, 1 Tbsp (15g)	4	2	13	3
1 Cup (239g)	60	37	209	48
Heavy Whipping, 1 Tbsp (15g)	6	4	21	5
1 Cup or 2 Cups Whipped (238g)	88	55	326	72
Light Whipping, 1 Tbsp (15g)	5	3	17	4
1 Cup or 2 Cups Whipped (239g)	74	46	265	60
Single, 1 Tbsp (15g)	2	1	6	1
1 Cup (242g)	28	17	89	22
Soured, Cultured, 1 Tbsp (12g)	3	2	5	2
1 Cup (230g)	48	30	102	35
Whipped				
2 Cups Heavy (238g)	88	55	326	72
2 Cups Light (239g)	74	46	265	60
Whipped, Pressurized				
1 Tbsp (3g)	1	0	2	1
1 Cup (60g)	13	8	46	11
Cream Puffs				
With Custard Filling, 1 Choux Pastry, 3½ In (130g)	18	6	187	15
Cream Substitute, Nondairy				
Powdered, 1 Tsp (2g)	1	1	0	1
With Hydrogenated Vegetable Oil and Soy Protein				
½ Cup (120g)	12	2	0	2
With Lauric Acid Oil and Sodium Caseinate				
½ Cup (120g)	12	11	0	11
Creamed Coconut				
1oz (28.4g)	20	17	0	18
3.5oz (100g)	69	61	0	62
Cress				
Garden, Fresh, ½ Cup (25g)	0	0	0	0
Crispbread, Rye				
Whole-grain, 10 Wafers (65g)	1	0	1	0
8oz Package (227g)	3	0	2	0
Crisps				
1oz Packet (28.4g)	10	3	0	3

	TOTAL FAT (g)	SATURATED FAT (g)	CHOLES- TEROL (mg)	CQ
Croissant				
With Butter, 1 Croissant	25	14	216	25
Crumpet				
With Butter, 1 Crumpet	6	2	13	3
Cucumber				
Fresh, 1 Cucumber, 8¼ In (301g)	0	0	0	0
Currants				
Black, Fresh, 1 Cup (112g)	1	0	0	0
Red and White, Fresh, 1 Cup (112g)	0	0	0	0
Zante, Dried, 1 Cup (144g)	0	0	0	0
Custard				
Baked, 1 Cup (265g)	15	7	278	21
Custard Marrow				
Boiled, 1 Cup, 1-in Pieces (160g)	1	0	0	0
Fresh, 1 Cup, 1-in Pieces (132g)	0	0	0	0
1 Marrow, 5¾ In (203g)	1	0	0	0
Custard Tart				
1 Small Tart (85g)	25	6	51	8
Dandelion Greens				
Boiled, 1 Cup Chopped (105g)	1	0	0	0
Fresh, 1 Cup Chopped (55g)	0	0	0	0
Danish Pastry				
1 Pastry (75g)	18	5	48	8
Dates				
Fresh and Dried, 10 Fruits (83g)	0	0	0	0
1 Cup Chopped (178g)	1	0	0	0
Dessert Topping				
Nondairy, Powder, 1.5oz (42.5g)	17	16	0	16
Nondairy, 1.5oz Powder Prepared with ½ Cup Whole Milk				
1 Cup (80g)	10	9	8	9
Nondairy, Pressurized, 1 Cup (70g)	16	13	0	13
Devilled Crab				
1 Cup (240g)	23	7	245	19

	TOTAL FAT (g)	SATURATED FAT (g)	CHOLES-TEROL (mg)	CU
Dhal				
Home Recipe, 1 Cup (210g)	15	2	0	2
Dock				
Boiled, ½ Cup Chopped (100g)	1	0	0	0
Fresh, ½ Cup Chopped (67g)	1	0	0	0
Doughnuts				
Cake Type, 1 Doughnut (58g)	11	3	35	4
Yeast, Glazed, 1 Doughnut (42g)	10	2	11	3
Yeast, Plain, 1 Doughnut (42g)	11	3	11	3
Dressed Crab				
1 Cup (220g)	17	9	308	24
DUCK				
Domesticated				
Meat and Skin, Roasted, 1 Portion (173g)	49	17	145	24
½ Duck (382g)	108	37	321	53
Meat and Skin, Raw, 1 Portion (287g)	113	38	218	49
½ Duck (634g)	249	84	482	109
Meat Only, Roasted, 1 Portion (100g)	11	4	89	9
½ Duck (221g)	25	9	197	19
Meat Only, Raw, 1 Portion (137g)	8	3	106	8
½ Duck (303g)	18	7	233	19
Liver, Raw, 1 Liver (44g)	2	1	227	12
Wild				
Meat and Skin, Raw, ½ Duck (270g)	41	14	216	25
Breast Meat Only, Raw, ½ Breast (83g)	4	1	64	4
Dumplings				
2 Dumplings (85g)	21	6	7	6
Eclair				
with Custard Filling and Chocolate Icing, 1 Eclair (100g)	14	4	136	11
Egg and Cheese Sandwich				
1 Sandwich (156g)	19	7	291	21
Egg Salad Sandwich				
1 Sandwich (153g)	24	8	264	21
Eggnog				
1 Cup (254g)	19	11	149	19

	TOTAL FAT (g)	SATURATED FAT (g)	CHOLES- TEROL (mg)	CO
Eggnog Flavour Mix				
Powder, 2 Heaped Tsp (28.4g)	0	0	3	0
Prepared with 1 Cup Milk and 2 Heaped Tsp				
Powder (272g)	8	5	33	7

EGGS

Chicken

	TOTAL FAT (g)	SATURATED FAT (g)	CHOLES- TEROL (mg)	CO
Dried Egg White				
Powder, 1 Cup sifted (107g)	0	0	0	0
Dried Egg Yolk				
Powder, 1 Tbsp (4g)	3	1	117	7
1 Cup sifted (67g)	41	12	1962	111
Dried Whole Egg				
1 Tbsp (5g)	2	1	96	5
1 Cup sifted (85g)	36	11	1631	92
Fresh Egg				
Raw, 1 Large Egg (50g)	6	2	274	15
White, Raw, 1 Large Egg White (33g)	0	0	0	0
Yolk, Raw, 1 Large Egg Yolk (17g)	6	2	272	15
Fried Egg				
1 Large Egg (46g)	6	2	246	15
Hard-boiled				
1 Large Egg (50g)	6	2	274	15
1 Cup, chopped (136g)	15	5	745	42
Omelette				
Home Recipe, 1-Egg Omelette (64g)	15	7	301	23
Poached Egg				
1 Large Egg (50g)	6	2	273	15
Scrambled				
1 Large Egg (64g)	7	3	248	15
1 Cup (220g)	24	10	854	52

Other Eggs

	TOTAL FAT (g)	SATURATED FAT (g)	CHOLES- TEROL (mg)	CO
Duck				
Whole, Fresh, Raw, 1 Egg (70g)	10	3	619	34
Goose				
Whole, Fresh, Raw, 1 Egg (144g)	19	5	1227	67
Quail				
Whole, Fresh, Raw, 1 Egg (9g)	1	0	76	4
Turkey				
Whole, Fresh, Raw, 1 Egg (79g)	9	3	737	40
Elderberries				
Fresh, 1 Cup (145g)	1	0	0	0

	TOTAL FAT (g)	SATURATED FAT (g)	CHOLES-TEROL (mg)	CQ
Endive				
Fresh, 1 Cup Chopped (50g)	0	0	0	0
1 Head (513g)	1	0	0	0
Falafel				
1 Falafel (17g)	3	0	0	0
3 Falafels (51g)	9	1	0	1

FAT
See also under Oils

	TOTAL FAT (g)	SATURATED FAT (g)	CHOLES-TEROL (mg)	CQ
Beef Dripping				
1 Tbsp (12.8g)	13	6	14	7
1 Cup (205g)	205	102	224	114
Butter				
Hard, 1 Pat (5g)	4	3	11	3
4oz (113.4g)	92	57	248	70
Whipped, 1 Pat (3.8g)	3	2	8	2
4oz (75.6g)	61	38	166	47
Chicken				
1 Tbsp (12.8g)	13	4	11	4
1 Cup (205g)	205	61	174	70
Duck				
1 Tbsp (12.8g)	13	4	13	5
1 Cup (205g)	205	68	205	79
Ghee (Butter Oil)				
1 Tbsp (12.8g)	13	8	33	10
1 Cup (205g)	204	127	525	154
Goose				
1 Tbsp (12.8g)	13	4	13	4
1 Cup (205g)	205	57	205	68
Lard				
1 Cup (205g)	205	80	195	91
1 Tbsp (12.8g)	13	5	12	6
Margarine – *See under* Margarine				
Mutton Tallow				
1 Tbsp (12.8g)	13	6	13	7
1 Cup (205g)	205	97	209	108
Shortening				
Lard and Vegetable Oil Blend, 1 Tbsp (12.8g)	13	5	7	6
1 Cup (205g)	205	83	115	89
Vegetable Only, 1 Tbsp (12.8g)	13	4	0	4
1 Cup (205g)	205	63	0	63
Turkey				
1 Tbsp (12.8g)	13	4	13	4
1 Cup (205g)	205	60	209	71

	TOTAL FAT (g)	SATURATED FAT (g)	CHOLES- TEROL (mg)	CQ
Fennel				
Leaves, Fresh, 3.5oz (100g)	0	0	0	0
Figs				
Candied, 3.5oz (100g)	0	0	0	0
Dried, Stewed, 1 Cup (259g)	1	0	0	0
Dried, Uncooked, 1 Cup (199g)	2	1	0	0
Fresh, 1 Fruit (50–65g)	0	0	0	0
Tinned, 1 Cup (248g)	0	0	0	0
Fish and Chips				
1 Portion (167g)	23	8	42	10
Fish Cakes				
Fried, 1 Regular Cake (60g)	5	2	25	3
Fish Fillet				
Battered or Breaded, Fried, 1 Fillet (91g)	11	3	31	4
Fish Fingers				
1 Finger (28g)	3	1	31	2
2 Fingers (57g)	7	2	64	5
Fish Loaf				
Cooked, 1 Slice (150g)	6	2	60	5
1 Whole Loaf (1215g)	45	12	486	37
Fish Sandwich				
With Tartar Sauce, 1 Sandwich (158g)	23	5	55	8
With Tartar Sauce and Cheese, 1 Sandwich (183g)	29	8	68	12

FISH and SHELLFISH

	TOTAL FAT (g)	SATURATED FAT (g)	CHOLES- TEROL (mg)	CQ
Abalone				
Fried, 3oz (85g)	6	1	80	5
Raw, 3oz (85g)	1	0	72	4
Anchovy				
Tinned in Oil, Drained Solids, 5 Anchovies (20g)	2	0	17	1
1 Tin (45g)	4	1	38	3
Raw, 3oz (85g)	4	1	51	4
Barracuda				
Raw, 3.5oz (100g)	3	1	55	4
Bass				
Raw, 3oz (85g)	2	0	68	4
Bluefish				
Raw, 3oz (85g)	4	1	50	3

	TOTAL FAT (g)	SATURATED FAT (g)	CHOLES-TEROL (mg)	CQ
Bream				
Braised or Stewed, 3oz (85g)	1	0	54	3
Raw, 3oz (85g)	2	1	43	3
Brill				
Poached or Grilled, 3oz (85g)	1	0	58	3
Raw, 3oz (85g)	1	0	41	2
Burbot				
Raw, 3oz (85g)	1	0	51	3
Carp				
Grilled or Baked, 3oz (85g)	6	1	71	5
Raw, 3oz (85g)	5	1	56	4
Catfish				
Breaded and Fried, 3oz (85g)	11	3	69	6
Raw, 3oz (85g)	4	1	49	3
Caviar				
Black and Red, Granular, 1 Tbsp (16g)	3	1	94	5
1oz (28g)	5	1	165	9
Clam				
Breaded and Fried, 3oz (85g)	10	2	52	5
20 Small Clams (188g)	21	5	115	11
Steamed or Boiled, 3oz (85g)	2	0	57	3
20 Small Clams (90g)	2	0	60	3
Tinned, Drained Solids, 3oz (85g)	2	0	57	3
1 Cup (160g)	3	0	107	6
Raw, 3oz (85g)	1	0	29	2
20 Small Clams (180g)	2	0	61	3
Cod				
Braised or Baked, 3oz (85g)	1	0	47	2
Dried and Salted, 3oz (85g)	2	0	129	7
Tinned, Solids and Liquid, 3oz (85g)	1	0	47	2
1 Tin (312g)	3	1	172	9
Raw, 3oz (85g)	1	0	37	2
Crab				
Blue, Steamed or Boiled, 3oz (85g)	2	0	85	4
Blue, Tinned, Drained Solids or Dry Pack, 3oz (85g)	1	0	76	4
Blue, Raw, 3oz (85g)	1	0	66	4
Devilled, 1 Cup (240g)	23	7	245	19
Dressed, 1 Cup (220g)	17	9	308	24
Imitation, made from Surimi (*see entry in this section*), 3oz (85g)	1	0	17	1
King, Steamed or Boiled, 3oz (85g)	1	0	45	2
King, Raw, 3oz (85g)	1	0	36	2
Crab Cakes				
1 Cake (60g)	5	1	90	5

	TOTAL FAT (g)	SATURATED FAT (g)	CHOLES- TEROL (mg)	CO
Crayfish				
Steamed or Boiled, 3oz (85g)	1	0	151	8
Raw, 3oz (85g)	1	0	118	6
Cuttlefish				
Raw, 3oz (85g)	1	0	95	5
Drumfish				
Breaded and Fried, 3oz (85g)	11	3	71	7
Raw, 3oz (85g)	3	1	52	4
Eel				
Grilled or Roasted, 3oz (85g)	13	3	137	9
Raw, 3oz (85g)	10	2	107	7
Fish Fingers				
Heated from Frozen, 1 Finger (28g)	3	1	31	2
Flounder				
Poached or Grilled, 3oz (85g)	1	0	58	3
Raw, 3oz (85g)	1	0	41	2
Grouper				
Poached or Grilled, 3oz (85g)	1	0	40	2
Raw, 3oz (85g)	1	0	32	2
Haddock				
Braised or Poached, 3oz (85g)	1	0	63	3
Smoked, 3oz (85g)	1	0	66	3
Raw, 3oz (85g)	1	0	49	3
Hake				
Braised or Baked, 3oz (85g)	1	0	47	2
Raw, 3oz (85g)	1	0	37	2
Halibut				
Grilled, Poached or Baked, 3oz (85g)	3	0	35	2
Raw, 3oz (85g)	2	0	27	2
Herring				
Grilled, 3oz (85g)	10	2	66	6
Kippered, 1 Fillet (40g)	5	1	33	3
Pickled, 1 Piece (15g)	3	0	2	0
Raw, 3oz (85g)	8	2	51	4
Kippers				
Grilled, 1 Fillet (40g)	5	1	33	3
Langouste				
Raw, 3oz (85g)	1	0	60	3
Ling				
Raw, 3oz (85g)	1	0	34	2
Lobster				
Steamed or Boiled, 3oz (85g)	1	0	61	3
In Newberg Sauce, 1 Cup (250g)	27	15	455	38
Raw, 3oz (85g)	1	0	81	4
Lobster Paste				
Tinned, 1 Tsp (7g)	1	0	12	1
3.5oz (100g)	9	5	172	14

	TOTAL FAT (g)	SATURATED FAT (g)	CHOLES- TEROL (mg)	CQ
Lobster Salad				
½ Cup (4oz) (260g)	17	3	120	9
Lox				
3oz (85g)	4	1	20	2
Lumpfish				
Raw, 3oz (85g)	2	0	35	2
Mackerel				
Grilled or Poached, 3oz (85g)	15	4	64	7
Raw, 3oz (85g)	12	3	60	6
Milkfish				
Raw, 3oz (85g)	6	1	44	4
Monkfish				
Raw, 3oz (85g)	1	0	21	1
Mullet				
Grilled or Baked, 3oz (85g)	4	1	54	4
Raw, 3oz (85g)	3	1	42	3
Mussel				
Steamed or Boiled, 3oz (85g)	4	1	48	3
Raw, 3oz (85g)	2	0	24	2
Octopus				
Raw, 3oz (85g)	1	0	41	2
Oyster				
Breaded and Fried, 6 Medium Oysters (88g)	11	3	71	6
3oz (85g)	11	3	69	6
Steamed or Boiled, 6 Medium Oysters (42g)	2	1	46	3
3oz (85g)	4	1	93	6
Tinned, 3oz (85g)	2	1	47	3
Raw, 6 Medium Oysters (84g)	2	1	46	3
Perch				
Stewed, 3oz (85g)	1	0	98	5
Raw, 3oz (85g)	1	0	77	4
Pike				
Braised, 3oz (85g)	1	0	43	2
Raw, 3oz (85g)	1	0	33	2
Pike-Perch				
Raw, 3oz (85g)	1	0	73	4
Plaice				
Poached or Grilled, 3oz (85g)	1	0	58	3
Raw, 3oz (85g)	1	0	41	2
Pollock				
Steamed or Baked, 3oz (85g)	1	0	82	4
Raw, 3oz (85g)	1	0	60	3
Prawn				
Breaded and Fried, 3oz (85g)	10	2	151	9
Steamed or Boiled, 3oz (85g)	1	0	166	9
Raw, 3oz (85g)	2	0	129	7

	TOTAL FAT (g)	SATURATED FAT (g)	CHOLES-TEROL (mg)	CQ
Roe				
Mixed Species, Raw, 1oz (28g)	2	0	105	6
3oz (85g)	6	1	318	17
Sablefish				
Smoked, 3oz (85g)	17	4	54	6
Raw, 3oz (85g)	13	3	42	5
Salmon				
Chum, Tinned, Drained Solids with Bone,				
3oz (85g)	5	1	33	3
1 Tin (369g)	20	6	144	13
Chum, Raw, 3oz (85g)	3	1	63	4
King, Smoked, 3oz (85g)	4	1	20	2
King, Raw, 3oz (85g)	9	2	56	5
Red, Tinned, Solids with Bone and Liquid,				
3oz (85g)	5	1	47	4
1 Tin (454g)	28	7	250	20
Red, Raw, 3oz (85g)	3	1	44	3
Sockeye, Grilled or Braised, 3oz (85g)	9	2	74	5
Sockeye, Tinned, Drained Solids with Bone,				
3oz (85g)	6	1	37	3
1 Tin (369g)	27	6	162	14
Sockeye, Raw, 3oz (85g)	7	1	53	4
Sardine				
Tinned in Oil, Drained Solids with Bone,				
2 Sardines (24g)	3	0	34	2
1 Tin (92g)	11	1	131	8
Tinned in Tomato Sauce, Drained Solids with Bone				
1 Sardine (38g)	5	1	23	2
1 Tin (370g)	44	11	226	23
Scallop				
Breaded and Fried, 2 Large Scallops (31g)	3	1	19	2
Imitation, made from Surimi (*see below*),				
3oz (85g)	0	0	19	1
Raw, 2 Large Scallops (30g)	0	0	10	1
3oz (85g)	1	0	28	1
Scampi				
Breaded and Fried, 4 Scampi (30g)	4	1	53	3
Raw, 4 Scampi (28g)	1	0	43	2
Sea Bass				
Poached, Grilled or Braised, 3oz (85g)	2	1	45	3
Raw, 3oz (85g)	2	0	35	2
Sea Bream				
Poached, Grilled or Steamed, 3oz (85g)	2	0	46	3
Raw, 3oz (85g)	1	0	36	2
Sea Perch				
Poached, Grilled or Braised, 3oz (85g)	2	1	45	3
Raw, 3oz (85g)	2	0	35	2

	TOTAL FAT (g)	SATURATED FAT (g)	CHOLES- TEROL (mg)	CQ
Sea Trout				
Raw, 3oz (85g)	3	1	71	4
Shad				
Raw, 3oz (85g)	12	4	64	7
Shark				
Batter-dipped and Fried, 3oz (85g)	12	3	50	5
Raw, 3oz (85g)	4	1	43	3
Sheepshead				
Braised or Stewed, 3oz (85g)	1	0	54	3
Raw, 3oz (85g)	2	1	43	3
Shrimp				
Breaded and Fried, 3oz (85g)	10	2	151	9
Imitation, made from Surimi (*see below*), 3oz (85g)	1	0	31	2
Steamed or Boiled, 3oz (85g)	1	0	166	9
Tinned, 3oz (85g)	2	0	147	8
Raw, 3oz (85g)	2	0	129	7
Shrimp Paste				
Tinned, 1 Tsp (7g)	1	0	12	1
3.5oz (100g)	9	5	172	14
Skate				
Poached or Grilled, 3oz (85g)	1	0	58	3
Raw, 3oz (85g)	1	0	41	2
Smelt				
Grilled, 3oz (85g)	3	1	77	4
Raw, 3oz (85g)	2	0	60	3
Sole				
Steamed or Baked, 3oz (85g)	1	0	58	3
Raw, 3oz (85g)	1	0	41	2
Sprat				
Grilled, 3oz (85g)	10	2	66	6
Raw, 3oz (85g)	8	2	51	4
Squid				
Fried, 3oz (85g)	6	2	221	13
Raw, 3oz (85g)	1	0	198	10
Sturgeon				
Baked, Grilled or Roasted, 3oz (85g)	4	1	66	4
Smoked, 3oz (85g)	4	1	68	4
Raw, 3oz (85g)	3	1	51	3
Sucker				
Raw, 3oz (85g)	2	0	35	2
Surimi				
Parts of Various Fish used to make Imitation Fish Products				
3oz (85g)	1	0	26	1
Swordfish				
Baked, Grilled or Poached, 3oz (85g)	4	1	43	3
Raw, 3oz (85g)	3	1	33	3

	TOTAL FAT (g)	SATURATED FAT (g)	CHOLES-TEROL (mg)	CO
Trout				
Poached or Braised, 3oz (85g)	4	1	62	4
Raw, 3oz (85g)	6	1	49	3
Tuna				
Fresh, Roasted or Grilled, 3oz (85g)	5	1	42	3
Fresh, Raw, 3oz (85g)	4	1	32	3
Tinned in Oil, Drained Solids, 3oz (85g)	7	1	26	3
1 Tin (178g)	14	3	55	6
Tinned in Water, Drained Solids, 3oz (85g)	2	1	36	2
1 Tin (172g)	4	1	72	5
Tuna Salad				
3oz (85g)	8	1	11	2
1 Cup (205g)	19	3	27	5
Turbot				
Raw, 3oz (85g)	3	1	41	3
Whelk				
Steamed or Boiled, 3oz (85g)	1	0	111	6
Raw, 3oz (85g)	0	0	55	3
Whitebait				
Smoked, 3oz (85g)	1	0	28	2
Raw, 3oz (85g)	5	1	51	3
Whiting				
Grilled or Poached, 3oz (85g)	1	0	71	4
Raw, 3oz (85g)	1	0	57	3
Zander				
Raw, 3oz (85g)	1	0	73	4

FLOUR

	TOTAL FAT (g)	SATURATED FAT (g)	CHOLES-TEROL (mg)	CO
Buckwheat				
Dark, 1 Cup (98g)	3	0	0	0
Light, 1 Cup (98g)	1	0	0	0
Carob				
1 Cup (103g)	1	0	0	0
Chestnut				
1 Cup (100g)	4	0	0	0
Cornflour				
1 Cup (117g)	3	0	0	0
Cottonseed				
Partially Defatted, 1 Cup (94g)	6	2	0	2
Peanut				
Defatted, 1 Cup (60g)	0	0	0	0
Low-fat, 1 Cup (60g)	13	2	0	2
Potato				
1 Cup (179g)	1	0	0	0
Rye				
Whole-grain, Dark, 1 Cup (128g)	3	0	0	0

	TOTAL FAT (g)	SATURATED FAT (g)	CHOLES- TEROL (mg)	CQ
Whole-grain, Light, 1 Cup (102g)	1	0	0	0
Whole-grain, Medium, 1 Cup (88g)	2	0	0	0
Sesame				
High-fat, 1oz (28.4g)	11	2	0	1
Low-fat, 1oz (28.4g)	1	0	0	0
Partially Defatted, 1oz (28.4g)	3	1	0	0
Soy				
Defatted, 1 Cup (100g)	1	0	0	0
Full-fat, Roasted, 1 Cup (85g)	19	3	0	3
Low-fat, 1 Cup (88g)	6	1	0	1
Sunflower Seed				
Partially Defatted, 1 Cup (80g)	1	0	0	0
Wheat				
80–85% Extraction, 1 Cup (100g)	1	0	0	0
All Purpose, 1 Cup (125g)	1	0	0	0
Bread, 1 Cup (137g)	2	0	0	0
Cake, 1 Cup (118g)	1	0	0	0
Gluten, 45% Gluten, 1 Cup (140g)	3	0	0	0
Self-raising, 1 Cup (125g)	1	0	0	0
Whole-wheat, 1 Cup (120g)	2	0	0	0
Frankfurters				
Beef, Boiled or Grilled, 1 Frankfurter (57g)	16	7	35	9
Beef and Pork, Boiled or Grilled, 1 Frankfurter (57g)	17	6	29	8
Chicken, Boiled or Grilled, 1 Frankfurter (45g)	9	3	46	5
Mixed Meat, Boiled or Grilled, 1 Frankfurter (56g)	15	6	35	8
Tinned, Boiled or Grilled, 1 Frankfurter (48g)	9	4	30	5
Turkey, Boiled or Grilled, 1 Frankfurter (45g)	8	3	48	5
Fried Chicken				
2 Pieces, Breast or Wing (163g)	30	8	149	15
2 Pieces, Drumstick or Thigh (148g)	27	7	165	15
Fried Fish				
Battered or Breaded, 1 Fillet (91g)	11	3	31	4
Fried Rice				
1 Serving (170g)	27	3	0	3
Special, with Chicken and Vegetables, 1 Serving (205g)	30	4	47	6
Frog's Legs				
Raw, 3.5oz (100g)	0	0	50	3

	TOTAL FAT (g)	SATURATED FAT (g)	CHOLES- TEROL (mg)	CO
Frozen Dinners				
Fried Chicken with Mixed Vegetables, 1 Serving (100g)	9	3	49	5
Roast Beef with Potatoes, Peas and Sweetcorn, 1 Serving (100g)	3	2	50	5
Fruit Cake				
Rich, 1 Slice (85g)	9	3	43	5
Rich, Iced, 1 Slice (100g)	12	3	40	5
Fruit Cocktail				
Tinned, 1 Cup (248g)	0	0	0	0
Fruit Punch Drink				
1 Glass (247g)	0	0	0	0
Tinned or Bottled, 1 Glass (186g)	0	0	0	0
Fruit Salad				
Tinned, 1 Cup (249g)	0	0	0	0
Tropical, Tinned, 1 Cup (257g)	0	0	0	0
Fruit				
See also under individual names				
Mixed, Dried, 1 Cup (255g)	1	0	0	0
Mixed, Frozen, 1 Cup, thawed (250g)	1	0	0	0
Mixed, Tinned, 1 Cup (255g)	0	0	0	0
Fuki – *See* Butterbur				
Garlic				
1 Clove (3g)	0	0	0	0
Garlic Granules or Powder				
1 Tsp (2.8g)	0	0	0	0
1 Tbsp (8.4g)	0	0	0	0
Gelatin				
Dessert, made with Water, Plain, 1 Cup (240g)	0	0	0	0
Dessert, made with Water and Fruit, 1 Cup (240g)	0	0	0	0
Dry, 1 Envelope (7g)	0	0	0	0
Ghee (Butter Oil)				
1 Tbsp (12.8g)	13	8	33	10
1 Cup (205g)	204	127	525	154

	TOTAL FAT (g)	SATURATED FAT (g)	CHOLES- TEROL (mg)	CQ
Gherkins				
1 Cup (170g)	0	0	0	0
Ginger Root				
Crystallized, 1oz (28g)	0	0	0	0
Fresh, Finely Sliced or Grated, 1 Tbsp (11g)	0	0	0	0
Gingerbread				
1 Piece (117g)	15	5	70	9
Gluten – *See under* Flour				
GOOSE				
Meat and Skin				
Roasted, 1 Portion (188g)	41	13	171	22
½ Goose (774g)	170	53	704	89
Raw, 1 Portion (320g)	108	31	256	44
½ Goose (1319g)	443	129	1055	183
Meat Only				
Roasted, 1 Portion (143g)	18	7	137	13
½ Goose (591g)	75	27	567	56
Raw, 1 Portion (185g)	13	5	155	13
½ Goose (766g)	55	21	643	54
Giblets				
Raw, 3.5oz (100g)	7	2	350	20
Gizzard				
Raw, 3.5oz (100g)	5	1	145	8
Liver Pâté				
Tinned, Smoked, 1 Tbsp (13g)	6	2	20	3
1oz (28.35g)	12	4	43	6
Liver				
Raw, 1 Liver (94g)	4	2	484	26
Gooseberries				
Fresh, 1 Cup (150g)	1	0	0	0
Tinned, 1 Cup (252g)	1	0	0	0
Gourd				
White-flowered, Boiled, 1 Cup, 1-in Cubes (146g)	0	0	0	0
Granadilla				
Fresh, 1 Fruit (18g)	0	0	0	0
Grape Juice				
Frozen Concentrate, Diluted, 1 Cup (250g)	0	0	0	0

	TOTAL FAT (g)	SATURATED FAT (g)	CHOLES- TEROL (mg)	CQ
Frozen Concentrate, Undiluted, 6 Fl.oz Container (216g)	1	0	0	0
Tinned or Bottled, 1 Cup (253g)	0	0	0	0
Grapefruit				
Juice, Frozen Concentrate, Diluted, 1 Cup (247g)	0	0	0	0
Juice, Frozen Concentrate, Undiluted, 6 Fl.oz Container (207g)	1	0	0	0
Fresh, 1 Cup Sections (247g)	0	0	0	0
1 Fruit with Juice (230g)	0	0	0	0
Tinned, 1 Cup Sections (250g)	0	0	0	0
Peel, Candied, 1oz (28g)	0	0	0	0
Grapes				
Fresh, 1 Cup (160g)	1	0	0	0
Tinned, 1 Cup (256g)	0	0	0	0

GRAVY

	TOTAL FAT (g)	SATURATED FAT (g)	CHOLES- TEROL (mg)	CQ
Au Jus				
Dehydrated, Prepared with Water, 1 Cup (246.1g)	1	0	0	0
Tinned, 1 Cup (238.4g)	1	0	0	0
1 Tin (298g)	1	0	0	0
Beef				
Tinned, 1 Cup (232.8g)	6	3	7	3
1 Tin (291g)	7	3	9	4
Brown				
Dehydrated, Prepared with Water, 1 Cup (260.6g)	0	0	0	0
Chicken				
Dehydrated, Prepared with Water, 1 Cup (259.7g)	2	1	3	1
Tinned, 1 Cup (238.4g)	14	3	5	4
1 Tin (298g)	17	4	6	5
Mushroom				
Dehydrated, Prepared with Water, 1 Cup (257.9g)	1	1	0	1
Tinned, 1 Cup (238.4g)	7	1	0	1
1 Tin (298g)	8	1	0	1
Onion				
Dehydrated, Prepared with Water, 1 Cup (261.4g)	1	1	0	0
Pork				
Dehydrated, Prepared with Water, 1 Cup (257.9g)	2	1	3	1
Turkey				

	TOTAL FAT (g)	SATURATED FAT (g)	CHOLES-TEROL (mg)	CO
Dehydrated, Prepared with Water, 1 Cup (261.4g)	2	1	3	1
Tinned, 1 Cup (238.4g)	5	2	5	2
1 Tin (298g)	6	2	6	2
Unspecified Type, Prepared with Water, 1 Cup (261.4g)	2	1	0	1

Guacamole (Avocado Dip)

Home Recipe, 4 tablespoons (60g)	8	6	0	6

Guava

1 Fruit (6g)	0	0	0	0
1 Cup Slices (244g)	2	0	0	0

Guava Sauce

Cooked, 1 Cup (238g)	0	0	0	0

Guinea Fowl

Meat and Skin, Raw, ½ Guinea (345g)	22	6	255	19
Meat Only, Raw, ½ Guinea (264g)	7	2	166	10
Giblets, Raw, 3.5oz (100g)	7	2	350	20

Ham
See also under Luncheon Meat, Pork

Devilled, Tinned, 4½oz Tin (128g)	41	15	83	19
1 Cup (225g)	73	26	146	34

Ham and Cheese Sandwich

1 Sandwich (146g)	15	6	58	9

Ham Croquette

1 Croquette (65g)	10	4	46	6

Ham, Egg and Cheese Sandwich

1 Sandwich (143g)	16	7	245	20

Ham Salad Spread

1oz (28.35g)	4	1	11	2

Ham Sandwich

1 Sandwich (140g)	12	5	43	7

Hamburger
See also under Beefburger, Cheeseburger

Plain, 1 Regular Patty (90g)	12	4	36	6
1 Large Patty (113g)	23	8	71	12

	TOTAL FAT (g)	SATURATED FAT (g)	CHOLES-TEROL (mg)	CQ
With Condiments and Vegetables, 1 Regular Patty (110g)	13	4	26	5
1 Large Patty (218g)	27	10	86	15
Double-decker with Condiments, 2 Regular Patties (215g)	32	12	102	17
2 Large Patties (259g)	41	16	142	23
Haws				
Scarlet, Fresh, 3.5oz (100g)	1	0	0	0
Hazelnuts				
Dried, 1oz (28.4g)	18	1	0	1
1 Cup Chopped Kernels (115g)	72	5	0	5
Honey				
1 Tbsp (21g)	0	0	0	0
1 Cup (339g)	0	0	0	0
Horseradish				
Prepared, 1 Tbsp (15g)	0	0	0	0
Horseradish-tree				
Pods, Boiled, 1 Cup Slices (118g)	0	0	0	0
Hot Chocolate				
Made with 1 Cup Milk and 2–3 Heaped Teaspoons Powder (266g)	9	6	32	7
Hot Dog				
Plain, 1 Hot-dog (98g)	17	6	29	8
Hot Pot				
Casserole, 1 Serving (340g)	14	6	85	10
Hummus				
1 Cup (246g)	21	3	0	3
Ice Cream				
French Vanilla, Soft Serve, 1 Cup (173g)	23	14	153	21
Vanilla, Approximately 10% Fat, 1 Cup (133g)	14	9	60	12
Vanilla, Approximately 16% Fat, 1 Cup (148g)	24	15	88	19
Sundae, Caramel, 1 Sundae (155g)	9	5	25	6
Sundae, Hot Fudge, 1 Sundae (158g)	9	5	21	6
Sundae, Strawberry, 1 Sundae (153g)	8	4	21	5

	TOTAL FAT (g)	SATURATED FAT (g)	CHOLES- TEROL (mg)	CQ
Ice Cream Cone				
3.5oz (100g)	2	1	0	1
Ice Milk				
Vanilla, 1 Cup (131g)	6	4	18	4
Vanilla, Softserve, 1 Cup (175g)	5	3	13	4
Ices				
Water, All Flavours, 1 Cup (193g)	0	0	0	0
Icing				
Chocolate Fudge, made with Butter, 1 Cup (310g)	45	19	62	22
Chocolate Fudge, made with Margarine, 1 Cup (310g)	45	11	0	11
Coconut, made from Dry Mix, 1 Cup (166g)	13	11	0	11
Creamy Fudge, made from Dry Mix, 1 Cup (245g)	16	5	0	5
Creamy Fudge, made with Butter, 1 Cup (245g)	37	17	71	21
Creamy Fudge, made with Margarine, 1 Cup (245g)	37	9	0	9
White, Boiled, 1 Cup (94g)	0	0	0	0
Jambul – *See* Java-plum				
Jams and Preserves				
1 Tbsp (20g)	0	0	0	0
1 Jar (284g)	0	0	0	0
Java-plum				
Fresh, 1 Cup (135g)	0	0	0	0
Jellies				
Fruit, 1 Tbsp (18g)	0	0	0	0
1 Cup (300g)	0	0	0	0
Jelly				
Made with Milk, 1 Serving (170g)	3	2	10	2
Made with Water, 1 Serving (170g)	0	0	0	0
Jicama				
Boiled, 3.5oz (100g)	0	0	0	0
Junket				
Chocolate, made from Mix with Milk, 1 Cup (255g)	10	5	31	7
Strawberry and Raspberry, made from Mix with Milk, 1 Cup (250g)	9	5	33	7

	TOTAL FAT (g)	SATURATED FAT (g)	CHOLES- TEROL (mg)	CO
Kale				
Boiled, 1 Cup Chopped (130g)	1	0	0	0
Fresh, 1 Cup Chopped (67g)	1	0	0	0
Katuray				
Fresh, 1 Cup Flowers (20g)	0	0	0	0
Steamed, 1 Cup Flowers (104g)	0	0	0	0
Kedgeree				
1 Serving (170g)	12	4	204	14
Kidney Beans				
Tinned, 1 Cup (256g)	1	0	0	0
Kippers				
Grilled, 1 Fillet (40g)	5	1	33	3
Kiwifruit				
Fresh, 1 Fruit (91g)	0	0	0	0
Kohlrabi				
Boiled, 1 Cup Slices (165g)	0	0	0	0
Kumquat				
Fresh, 1 Fruit (19g)	0	0	0	0

Lager – *See under* Alcohol

LAMB

Best-End
Choice
Fat, Raw, 3.5oz (100g)	77	43	75	47
Lean and Fat, Raw, 3.5oz (100g)	30	17	71	21
Lean, Grilled, 3.5oz (100g)	11	6	100	11
Lean, Raw, 3.5oz (100g)	8	5	70	8

Good
Fat, Raw, 3.5oz (100g)	74	41	75	46
Lean and Fat, Raw, 3.5oz (100g)	27	15	71	19
Lean, Grilled, 3.5oz (100g)	10	6	100	11
Lean, Raw, 3.5oz (100g)	8	4	70	8

Prime
Fat, Raw, 3.5oz (100g)	84	47	75	51
Lean and Fat, Raw, 3.5oz (100g)	41	23	71	27
Lean, Grilled, 3.5oz (100g)	12	7	100	12
Lean, Raw, 3.5oz (100g)	10	5	70	9

	TOTAL FAT (g)	SATURATED FAT (g)	CHOLES-TEROL (mg)	CQ
Chops				
Choice				
Lean and Fat, Grilled, 3.1oz (89g)	32	18	87	22
Loin, Lean and Fat, Grilled, 3.5oz (100g)	28	16	93	20
Good				
Lean and Fat, Grilled, 3.5oz (100g)	32	18	98	23
Loin, Lean and Fat, Grilled, 3.5oz (100g)	27	15	98	20
Prime				
Lean and Fat, Grilled, 3.5oz (100g)	47	26	98	31
Loin, Lean and Fat, Grilled, 3.5oz (100g)	37	21	98	26
Composite Cuts				
Choice, Raw, Lean and Fat, 3.5oz (100g)	21	12	71	16
Good, Raw, Lean and Fat, 3.5oz (100g)	19	11	71	15
Prime, Raw, Lean and Fat, 3.5oz (100g)	27	15	71	19
Fat				
Cooked, 3.5oz (100g)	76	42	75	47
Heart				
Braised, 1 Cup (145g)	21	13	397	33
Raw, 3.5oz (100g)	10	6	150	14
Kidneys				
Raw, 3.5oz (100g)	3	1	375	20
Leg				
Choice				
Lean and Fat, Roasted, 3.5oz (100g)	20	11	104	17
Lean and Fat, Raw, 3.5oz (100g)	16	9	71	13
Lean, Roasted, 3.5oz (100g)	8	4	111	10
Lean, Raw, 3.5oz (100g)	5	3	70	6
Good				
Lean and Fat, Roasted, 3.5oz (100g)	17	10	98	15
Lean and Fat, Raw, 3.5oz (100g)	15	8	71	12
Lean, Roasted, 3.5oz (100g)	7	4	100	9
Lean, Raw, 3.5oz (100g)	5	3	70	6
Prime				
Lean and Fat, Roasted, 3.5oz (100g)	24	13	98	18
Lean and Fat, Raw, 3.5oz (100g)	21	12	71	15
Lean, Roasted, 3.5oz (100g)	8	4	100	9
Lean, Raw, 3.5oz (100g)	6	3	70	7
Liver				
Grilled, 1.6oz Slice (45g)	6	1	197	11
Raw, 3.5oz (100g)	4	1	300	16

	TOTAL FAT (g)	SATURATED FAT (g)	CHOLES- TEROL (mg)	CQ
Loin				
Choice				
Lean, Grilled, 3.5oz (100g)	7	4	98	9
Lean, Raw, 3.5oz (100g)	6	3	70	7
Good				
Lean, Grilled, 3.5oz (100g)	7	4	100	9
Lean, Raw, 3.5oz (100g)	6	3	70	7
Prime				
Lean, Grilled, 3.5oz (100g)	9	5	100	10
Lean, Raw, 3.5oz (100g)	7	4	70	7
Lungs				
Raw, 3.5oz (100g)	2	1	150	9
Shoulder				
Choice				
Lean and Fat, Roasted, 3.5oz (100g)	29	16	104	21
Lean and Fat, Raw, 3.5oz (100g)	24	13	71	17
Good				
Lean and Fat, Roasted, 3.5oz (100g)	25	14	98	19
Lean and Fat, Raw, 3.5oz (100g)	22	12	71	16
Lean, Roasted, 3.5oz (100g)	10	5	100	10
Lean, Raw, 3.5oz (100g)	7	4	70	8
Prime				
Lean and Fat, Roasted, 3.5oz (100g)	32	18	98	23
Lean and Fat, Raw, 3.5oz (100g)	28	16	71	20
Lean, Roasted, 3.5oz (100g)	11	6	100	11
Lean, Raw, 3.5oz (100g)	9	5	70	8
Spleen				
Raw, 3.5oz (100g)	4	1	250	14
Sweetbreads				
Braised, 3oz (85g)	5	2	396	22
Raw, 3.5oz (100g)	4	1	250	14
Tongue				
Braised, 1 Slice (20g)	4	2	20	3
Raw, 3.5oz (100g)	15	9	70	13
Lamb's Lettuce				
Fresh, 1 Cup (56g)	0	0	0	0
Lamb's Quarters				
Boiled, 1 Cup Chopped (180g)	1	0	0	0

	TOTAL FAT (g)	SATURATED FAT (g)	CHOLES- TEROL (mg)	CQ
Lard				
1 Tbsp (12.8g)	13	5	12	6
1 Cup (205g)	205	80	195	91
Leeks				
Boiled, 1 Leek (124g)	0	0	0	0
Fresh, 1 Leek (124g)	0	0	0	0
Lemon				
Fresh, 1 Fruit (108g)	0	0	0	0
Lemon Curd				
2 Tablespoons (45g)	6	3	68	7
Lemon Juice				
Fresh, 1 Tbsp (15.2g)	0	0	0	0
1 Cup (244g)	0	0	0	0
Tinned or Bottled, 1 Tbsp (15.2g)	0	0	0	0
1 Cup (244g)	1	0	0	0
Lemon Peel				
Candied, 1oz (28g)	0	0	0	0
Fresh, 1 Tbsp (6g)	0	0	0	0
Lemonade Flavour Drink				
Prepared with Water, 1 Cup Water and 2 Tbsp Powder (266g)	0	0	0	0
Lemonade				
Frozen Concentrate, 6 Fl.oz Tin (219g)	0	0	0	0
Frozen Concentrate, Diluted, 1 Cup (248g)	0	0	0	0
Lentils				
See also under Beans and Pulses				
Boiled, 1 Cup (198g)	1	0	0	0
Fresh, 1 Cup (192g)	2	0	0	0
Sprouted, Fresh, 1 Cup (77g)	0	0	0	0
Sprouted, Stir-fried, 3.5oz (100g)	1	0	0	0
Lettuce				
Cos or Romaine, Fresh, 1 Inner Leaf (10g)	0	0	0	0
Iceberg (includes Crisphead Types), Fresh, 1 Leaf (20g)	0	0	0	0
Looseleaf, Fresh, 1 Leaf (10g)	0	0	0	0
Roundhead (includes Butterhead Types), Fresh, 1 Leaf (10g)	0	0	0	0

	TOTAL FAT (g)	SATURATED FAT (g)	CHOLES-TEROL (mg)	CQ
Lime				
Fresh, 1 Fruit (67g)	0	0	0	0
Juice, Fresh, 1 Tbsp (15.4g)	0	0	0	0
1 Cup (246g)	0	0	0	0
Juice, Tinned or Bottled, 1 Tbsp (15.4g)	0	0	0	0
1 Cup (246g)	1	0	0	0
Limeade				
Frozen Concentrate, 6 Fl.oz Tin (218g)	0	0	0	0
Frozen Concentrate, Diluted, 1 Cup (247g)	0	0	0	0
Lobster in Newberg Sauce				
1 Cup (250g)	27	15	455	38
Lobster Paste, Tinned				
1 Tsp (7g)	1	0	12	1
3.5oz (100g)	9	5	172	14
Lobster Salad				
½ Cup (260g)	17	3	120	9
Loganberries				
1 Cup (147g)	1	0	0	0
Longans				
Dried, 3.5oz (100g)	0	0	0	0
Fresh, 3.5oz (100g)	0	0	0	0
Loquats				
Fresh, 1 Fruit (9.9g)	0	0	0	0
Lotus Root				
Boiled, 10 Slices (89g)	0	0	0	0
Fresh, 10 Slices (81g)	0	0	0	0

LUNCHEON MEAT

	TOTAL FAT (g)	SATURATED FAT (g)	CHOLES-TEROL (mg)	CQ
Beef				
Loaved, 1 Slice (28.35g)	7	3	18	4
Thin Sliced, 1oz (28.35g)	1	1	12	1
Corned Beef Loaf				
Jellied, 1 Slice (28.35g)	2	1	13	1
Ham				
Chopped, Pressed, 1 Slice (28.35g)	5	2	15	2
Chopped, Spiced, Tinned, 1 Slice (28.35g)	5	2	14	2
Extra Lean (5% Fat), 1 Slice (28.35g)	1	1	13	1

	TOTAL FAT (g)	SATURATED FAT (g)	CHOLES-TEROL (mg)	CO
Lean (11% Fat), 1 Slice (28.35g)	3	1	16	2
Minced, 1 Slice (28.35g)	6	2	20	3
Ham Salad Spread				
1oz (28.35g)	4	1	11	2
Peppered Loaf				
Pork and Beef, 1 Slice (28.35g)	2	1	13	1
Pickle and Pimiento Loaf				
Pork, 1 Slice (28.35g)	6	2	11	3
Picnic Loaf				
1 Slice (28.35g)	5	2	11	2
Pork and Beef				
Chopped Together, 1 Slice (28.35g)	9	3	16	4
Pork				
Tinned, 1 Slice (28.35g)	9	3	18	4
Turkey Loaf				
1 Slice (28.35g)	4	1	28	3
Lychees				
Dried, 3.5oz (100g)	1	0	0	0
Fresh, 1 Cup (190g)	1	0	0	0
Macaroni				
Boiled, 1 Cup (140g)	1	0	0	0
Macaroni Cheese				
Made with Butter, 1 Cup (200g)	22	12	68	15
Made with Margarine, 1 Cup (200g)	22	9	42	11
Tinned, 1 Cup (240g)	10	4	24	5
1 Tin (430g)	17	8	43	10
Malt Extract				
1oz (28g)	0	0	0	0
Malt				
Dry, 1oz (28g)	1	0	0	0
Malted Milk Flavour Mix				
Chocolate, 4–5 Heaping Tsp (21g)	1	0	1	0
Chocolate, made with 1 Cup Milk and 4–5 Heaping Tsp				
Powder (265g)	9	6	35	7
Natural, 3 Heaping Tsp (21g)	2	1	4	1
Natural, made with 1 Cup Milk and 3 Heaping Tsp				
Powder (265g)	10	6	37	8

	TOTAL FAT (g)	SATURATED FAT (g)	CHOLES- TEROL (mg)	CO
Mandarin Orange				
Fresh, 1 Fruit (84g)	0	0	0	0
1 Cup Sections (195g)	0	0	0	0
Tinned, 1 Cup Sections (249g)	0	0	0	0
Mange-tout – *see* Peas (Edible-pod)				
Mango				
Fresh, 1 Fruit (207g)	1	0	0	0

MARGARINE

Diet Spreads (40% Fat)

	TOTAL FAT (g)	SATURATED FAT (g)	CHOLES- TEROL (mg)	CO
Corn (Hydrogenated and Regular)				
1 Tsp (4.8g)	2	0	0	0
1 Cup (232g)	90	15	0	15
Soybean (Hydrogenated)				
1 Tsp (4.8g)	2	0	0	0
1 Cup (232g)	90	15	0	15
Soybean and Cottonseed				
1 Tsp (4.8g)	2	0	0	0
1 Cup (232g)	90	19	0	19
Soybean and Cottonseed (Hydrogenated)				
1 Tsp (4.8g)	2	0	0	0
1 Cup (232g)	90	17	0	17
Soybean and Palm (Hydrogenated and Regular)				
1 Tsp (4.8g)	2	1	0	0
1 Cup (232g)	90	23	0	24
Unspecified Oils				
1 Tsp (4.8g)	2	0	0	0
1 Cup (232g)	90	18	0	18

Low-fat Spreads (60% Fat)

	TOTAL FAT (g)	SATURATED FAT (g)	CHOLES- TEROL (mg)	CO
Soybean (Hydrogenated) and Palm (Hydrogenated)				
1 Tsp (4.8g)	3	1	0	1
1 Cup (229g)	139	32	0	33
Soybean (Hydrogenated) and Cottonseed (Hydrogenated)				
1 Tsp (4.8g)	3	1	0	1
1 Cup (229g)	139	28	0	28
Soybean (Hydrogenated) and Palm (Hydrogenated and Regular)				
1 Tsp (4.8g)	3	1	0	1
1 Cup (229g)	139	31	0	31

	TOTAL FAT (g)	SATURATED FAT (g)	CHOLES- TEROL (mg)	CO
Unspecified Oils				
1 Tsp (4.8g)	3	1	0	1
1 Cup (229g)	139	29	0	30

Hard Block (80% Fat)

	TOTAL FAT (g)	SATURATED FAT (g)	CHOLES- TEROL (mg)	CO
Coconut (Hydrogenated and Regular) and Safflower and Palm (Hydrogenated)				
1 Tsp (4.7g)	4	3	0	3
1 Block (113.4g)	91	65	0	65
Corn and Soybean (Hydrogenated) and Cottonseed (Hydrogenated)				
1 Tsp (4.7g)	4	1	0	1
1 Block (113.4g)	91	17	0	17
Corn (Hydrogenated and Regular)				
1 Tsp (4.7g)	4	1	0	1
1 Block (113.4g)	91	16	0	16
Lard (Hydrogenated)				
1 Tsp (4.7g)	4	2	2	2
1 Block (113.4g)	91	36	58	39
Safflower and Soybean (Hydrogenated)				
1 Tsp (4.7g)	4	1	0	1
1 Block (113.4g)	91	16	0	16
and Cottonseed (Hydrogenated)				
1 Tsp (4.7g)	4	1	0	1
1 Block (113.4g)	91	15	0	15
Safflower and Soybean (Hydrogenated and Regular) and Cottonseed (Hydrogenated)				
1 Tsp (4.7g)	4	1	0	1
1 Block (113.4g)	91	16	0	16
Soybean (Hydrogenated and Regular)				
1 Tsp (4.7g)	4	1	0	1
1 Block (113.4g)	91	15	0	15
Soybean (Hydrogenated) and Corn and Cottonseed (Hydrogenated)				
1 Tsp (4.7g)	4	1	0	1
1 Block (113.4g)	91	23	0	23
Soybean (Hydrogenated) and Cottonseed (Hydrogenated)				
1 Tsp (4.7g)	4	1	0	1
1 Block (113.4g)	91	18	0	18
Soybean (Hydrogenated) and Palm (Hydrogenated and Regular)				
1 Tsp (4.7g)	4	1	0	1
1 Block (113.4g)	91	20	0	20
Sunflower and Soybean (Hydrogenated) and Cottonseed (Hydrogenated)				
1 Tsp (4.7g)	4	1	0	1
1 Block (113.4g)	91	14	0	14

	TOTAL FAT (g)	SATURATED FAT (g)	CHOLES- TEROL (mg)	CQ
Unspecified Oils				
1 Tsp (4.7g)	4	1	0	1
1 Block (113.4g)	91	18	0	18

Soft Tub (80% Fat)

	TOTAL FAT (g)	SATURATED FAT (g)	CHOLES- TEROL (mg)	CQ
Corn (Hydrogenated and Regular)				
1 Tsp (4.7g)	4	1	0	1
1 Cup (227g)	183	32	0	32
Safflower and Cottonseed (Hydrogenated) and Peanut (Hydrogenated)				
1 Tsp (4.7g)	4	1	0	1
1 Cup (227g)	183	30	0	31
Safflower (Hydrogenated and Regular)				
1 Tsp (4.7g)	4	0	0	0
1 Cup (227g)	183	21	0	21
Soybean (Hydrogenated and Regular)				
1 Tsp (4.7g)	4	1	0	1
1 Cup (227g)	183	31	0	31
Soybean (Hydrogenated) and Cottonseed (Hydrogenated)				
1 Tsp (4.7g)	4	1	0	1
1 Cup (227g)	183	35	0	35
Soybean (Hydrogenated) and Cottonseed				
1 Tsp (4.7g)	4	1	0	1
1 Cup (227g)	183	38	0	38
Soybean (Hydrogenated) and Palm (Hydrogenated and Regular)				
1 Tsp (4.7g)	4	1	0	1
1 Cup (227g)	183	39	0	39
Soybean (Hydrogenated) and Safflower				
1 Tsp (4.7g)	4	1	0	0
1 Cup (227g)	183	24	0	24
Sunflower and Cottonseed (Hydrogenated) and Peanut (Hydrogenated)				
1 Tsp (4.7g)	4	1	0	1
1 Cup (227g)	183	29	0	29
Unspecified Oils				
1 Tsp (4.7g)	4	1	0	1
1 Cup (227g)	182	31	0	32

	TOTAL FAT (g)	SATURATED FAT (g)	CHOLES- TEROL (mg)	CQ
Marmalade				
Citrus, 3.5oz (100g)	0	0	0	0

	TOTAL FAT (g)	SATURATED FAT (g)	CHOLES- TEROL (mg)	CQ
Marrow				
Boiled, 1 Cup Slices (180g)	1	0	0	0
Fresh, 1 Cup Slices (130g)	0	0	0	0

	TOTAL FAT (g)	SATURATED FAT (g)	CHOLES-TEROL (mg)	CO
Marzipan				
1oz (28.4g)	8	1	0	1
1 Cup Firmly Packed (227g)	62	6	0	6
Matzos				
Crackers, 10 Crackers (33g)	6	2	0	2
Mayonnaise				
See also under Salad Dressing				
Imitation, made with Milk Cream, 1 Tbsp (15.0g)	1	0	7	1
1 Cup (240g)	12	7	103	12
Imitation, made with Egg and Soybean Oil,				
1 Tbsp (15.0g)	3	1	4	1
1 Cup (240g)	46	8	58	11
Imitation, made without Egg or Milk, made with Soybean Oil				
1 Tbsp (14.0g)	7	1	0	1
1 Cup (225g)	107	17	0	17
Made with Egg and Soybean and Safflower Oil,				
1 Tbsp (13.8g)	11	1	8	2
1 Cup (220g)	175	19	130	26
Made with Egg and Soybean Oil, 1 Tbsp (13.8g)	11	2	8	2
1 Cup (220g)	175	26	130	33
Meatloaf				
Home Recipe, 3.5oz (100g)	13	6	65	9
Melon Balls				
1 Cup (173g)	0	0	0	0
Melons				
Cantaloupe, Fresh, ½ Fruit (267g)	1	0	0	0
Casaba, Fresh, 1/10 Fruit (164g)	0	0	0	0
Honeydew, Fresh, 1/10 Fruit (129g)	0	0	0	0

MILK

Cow's Milk

Buttermilk

	TOTAL FAT (g)	SATURATED FAT (g)	CHOLES-TEROL (mg)	CO
Dried, 1 Tbsp (6.5g)	0	0	5	0
1 Cup (120g)	7	4	83	9
Fluid, Cultured, 1 Cup (245g)	2	1	9	2
Chocolate Milk Drink				
1% Fat, 1 Cup (250g)	3	2	7	2
2% Fat, 1 Cup (250g)	5	3	17	4
Whole Milk, 1 Cup (250g)	9	5	31	7

	TOTAL FAT (g)	SATURATED FAT (g)	CHOLES- TEROL (mg)	CQ
Condensed				
Tinned, 1 Fl.oz (38.2g)	3	2	13	3
1 Cup (306g)	27	17	104	22
Dry				
Skimmed, Non-fat Solids, 2oz (60g)	0	0	12	1
Whole, 2oz (60g)	17	11	62	14
Evaporated				
Skimmed, Tinned, 1 Fl.oz (31.9g)	0	0	1	0
1 Cup (256g)	1	0	9	1
Whole, Tinned, 1 Fl.oz (31.5g)	2	1	9	2
1 Cup (252g)	19	12	74	15
Low-fat				
1% Fat, 1 Cup (244g)	3	2	10	2
2% Fat, 1 Cup (244g)	5	3	18	4
Malted				
Beverage, 1 Cup Milk and 2–3 Tsp Powder (265g)	10	6	37	8
Chocolate Flavour, Beverage, 1 Cup Milk and 2–3 Tsp Powder (265g)	9	6	35	7
Dry Powder, 2–3 Tsp (21g)	2	1	4	1
Dry Powder, Chocolate, 2–3 Tsp (21g)	1	1	1	1
Skimmed				
1 Cup (245g)	0	0	4	0
Whole				
1 Cup (244g)	8	5	33	7

Other Milks

Coconut Milk (Liquid Expressed from Grated Meat and Water)				
Frozen, 1 Cup (240g)	50	44	0	45
Fresh, 1 Cup (240g)	57	51	0	51
Tinned, 1 Cup (226g)	48	43	0	43
Goat				
1 Cup (244g)	10	7	28	8
Human				
1 fl.oz (30.8g)	1	1	4	1
1 Cup (246g)	11	5	34	7
Sheep				
1 Cup (245g)	17	11	66	15
Soy				
1 Cup (240g)	5	1	0	1
Milk Shakes				
Chocolate, 10 Fl.oz (283g)	11	7	37	8
Strawberry, 10 Fl.oz (283g)	8	5	31	7
Vanilla, 10 Fl.oz (283g)	9	5	31	7

	TOTAL FAT (g)	SATURATED FAT (g)	CHOLES- TEROL (mg)	CQ
Milk Substitute				
Fluid made with Hydrogenated Vegetable Oils, 1 Cup (244g)	8	2	1	2
Fluid made with Lauric Acid Oil, 1 Cup (244g)	8	7	1	8
Millet				
Whole Grain, 3.5oz (100g)	3	1	0	1
Miso				
½ Cup (138g)	8	1	0	1
Molasses				
1 Cup (328g)	0	0	0	0
Moussaka				
Home Recipe, 1 Serving (225g)	30	11	90	15
Mulberries				
Fresh, 1 Cup (140g)	1	0	0	0
Mushrooms				
Boiled, 1 Cup Pieces (156g)	1	0	0	0
Fresh, 1 Cup Pieces (70g)	0	0	0	0
Shiitake, Cooked, 4 Mushrooms (72g)	0	0	0	0
1 Cup Pieces (145g)	0	0	0	0
Shiitake, Dried, 4 Mushrooms (15g)	0	0	0	0
Tinned, Drained Solids, 1 Cup Pieces (156g)	0	0	0	0
Mustard				
Prepared, Brown, 3.5oz (100g)	6	1	0	1
Prepared, Yellow, 3.5oz (100g)	4	0	0	0
Mustard Greens				
Boiled, 1 Cup Chopped (140g)	0	0	0	0
Fresh, 1 Cup Chopped (56g)	0	0	0	0
Nachos				
With Cheese, 1 Serving (113g)	19	8	18	9
With Cheese, Beans and Beef, 1 Serving (255g)	31	12	21	14
Natal-plum				
Fresh, 1 Fruit (20g)	0	0	0	0
Natto				
Fermented Soybean Paste, 1 Cup (175g)	19	3	0	3

	TOTAL FAT (g)	SATURATED FAT (g)	CHOLES- TEROL (mg)	CQ
Nectarine				
Fresh, 1 Fruit (136g)	1	0	0	0
Noodles				
Chow Mein, Tinned, 5oz Tin (142g)	33	9	17	9
1 Cup (45g)	11	3	5	3
Egg Noodles, Cooked, 1 Cup (160g)	2	0	50	2

NUT and SEED BUTTERS

	TOTAL FAT (g)	SATURATED FAT (g)	CHOLES- TEROL (mg)	CQ
Almond Butter				
1 Tbsp (16g)	9	1	0	1
1 Cup (250g)	148	14	0	14
Cashew Butter				
1 Tbsp (16g)	8	2	0	2
1 Cup (227g)	112	22	0	22
Peanut Butter				
1 Tbsp (16g)	8	2	0	2
1 Cup (258g)	129	25	0	25
Sesame Seed Paste				
1 Tbsp (16g)	8	1	0	1
1 Cup (227g)	116	16	0	16
Sunflower Seed Butter				
1 Tbsp(16g)	8	1	0	1
1 Cup (227g)	108	11	0	11
Tahini (From Ground Sesame Seeds)				
1 Tbsp (15g)	7	1	0	1
1 Cup (227g)	109	15	0	15

NUTS

See also under Seeds

	TOTAL FAT (g)	SATURATED FAT (g)	CHOLES- TEROL (mg)	CQ
Almonds				
Dried, Blanched, 1oz (26 Kernels) (28.4g)	15	1	0	1
1 Cup Kernels (145g)	76	7	0	7
Dried, Unblanched, 1oz (24 Kernels) (28.4g)	15	1	0	1
1 Cup Kernels (142g)	74	7	0	7
Dry Roasted, 1oz (28.4g)	15	1	0	1
1 Cup Kernels (138g)	71	7	0	7
Finely Ground, Full-fat, 1oz (28.4g)	15	1	0	1
1 Cup (65g)	34	3	0	3
Finely Ground, Partially Defatted, 1oz (28.4g)	5	0	0	0
1 Cup Not Packed (65g)	10	1	0	1
Oil Roasted, Blanched, 1oz (24 Whole Kernels) (28.4g)	16	2	0	2
1 Cup Whole Kernels (142g)	80	8	0	8

	TOTAL FAT (g)	SATURATED FAT (g)	CHOLES-TEROL (mg)	CQ
Oil Roasted, Unblanched, 1oz (22 Whole Kernels)				
(28.4g)	16	2	0	2
1 Cup Whole Kernels (157g)	91	9	0	9
Brazilnuts				
1oz (6–8 Kernels) (28.4g)	19	5	0	5
1 Cup (32 Kernels) (140g)	93	23	0	23
Cashew Nuts				
Dry Roasted, 1oz (28.4g)	13	3	0	3
1 Cup Whole and Halves (137g)	64	13	0	13
Oil Roasted, 1oz (28.4g)	14	3	0	3
1 Cup Whole and Halves (130g)	63	12	0	13
Chestnuts				
Boiled and Steamed, 1oz (28.4g)	0	0	0	0
1 Cup (145g)	2	0	0	0
Dried, Unpeeled, 1oz (28.4g)	1	0	0	0
1 Cup (100g)	4	1	0	1
Fresh, Unpeeled, 1oz (28.4g)	1	0	0	0
1 Cup (145g)	3	1	0	1
Roasted, 1oz (28.4g)	1	0	0	0
1 Cup (143g)	3	1	0	1
Coconuts				
Cream, Fresh (Liquid Expressed from Grated				
Meat), 1 Tbsp (15g)	5	5	0	5
1 Cup (240g)	83	74	0	75
Cream, Tinned, 1 Tbsp (19g)	3	3	0	3
1 Cup (296g)	53	47	0	47
Meat, Dried (Desiccated), 1oz (28.4g)	18	16	0	16
3.5oz (100g)	65	57	0	58
Meat, Dried (Desiccated), Creamed, 1oz (28.4g)	20	17	0	18
3.5oz (100g)	69	61	0	62
Meat, Dried (Desiccated), Flaked, 1oz (28.4g)	9	8	0	8
1 Cup (77g)	24	22	0	22
Meat, Dried (Desiccated), Shredded, 1oz (28.4g)	10	9	0	9
1 Cup (93g)	33	29	0	30
Meat, Dried (Desiccated), Toasted, 1oz (28.4g)	13	12	0	12
3.5oz (100g)	47	42	0	42
Meat, Fresh, 1 Piece (45g)	15	13	0	13
1 Cup Grated (80g)	27	24	0	24
Milk, Frozen (Liquid Expressed from Grated Meat				
and Water)				
1 Cup (240g)	50	44	0	45
Milk, Fresh, 1 Cup (240g)	57	51	0	51
Milk, Tinned, 1 Cup (226g)	48	43	0	43
Water (Liquid from Coconuts), 1 Cup (240g)	1	0	0	0
Filberts – see Hazelnuts below				
Ginkgo Nuts				
Dried, 1oz (28.4g)	1	0	0	0

	TOTAL FAT (g)	SATURATED FAT (g)	CHOLES-TEROL (mg)	CQ
3.5oz (100g)	2	0	0	0
Fresh, 1oz (28.4g)	1	0	0	0
3.5oz (100g)	2	0	0	0
Tinned, 1oz (14 Medium Kernels) (28.4g)	1	0	0	0
1 Cup (155g)	3	1	0	0
Hazelnuts				
Blanched, 1oz (28.4g)	19	1	0	1
1 Cup Kernels (115g)	67	5	0	5
Dried, Unblanched, 1oz (28.4g)	18	1	0	1
1 Cup Chopped Kernels (115g)	72	5	0	5
Dry Roasted, 1oz (28.4g)	19	1	0	1
1 Cup Kernels (115g)	66	5	0	5
Oil Roasted, 1oz (28.4g)	18	1	0	1
1 Cup Kernels (115g)	64	5	0	5
Macadamia Nuts				
1oz (28.4g)	21	3	0	3
1 Cup (134g)	99	15	0	15
Oil Roasted, 1oz (10–12 Kernels) (28.4g)	22	3	0	3
1 Cup Whole or Halves (134g)	103	15	0	16
Mixed Nuts				
Dry Roasted, 1oz (28.4g)	15	2	0	2
1 Cup (137g)	71	10	0	10
Oil Roasted, 1oz (28.4g)	16	3	0	3
1 Cup (142g)	80	12	0	13
Peanuts				
1oz (28.4g)	14	2	0	2
1 Cup (146g)	72	10	0	10
Oil Roasted, 1oz (28.4g)	14	2	0	2
1 Cup (144g)	71	10	0	10
Pecans				
Fresh, 1oz (20 Halves) (28.4g)	19	2	0	2
1 Cup (Halves) (108g)	73	6	0	6
Dry Roasted, 1oz (28.4g)	18	2	0	1
1 Cup (100g)	65	5	0	5
Oil Roasted, 1oz (15 Halves) (28.4g)	20	2	0	2
1 Cup (110g)	78	6	0	6
Pine Nuts				
1oz (28.4g)	17	3	0	3
3.5oz (100g)	61	9	0	9
Pistachio Nuts				
Fresh, 1oz (47 Kernels) (28.4g)	14	2	0	2
1 Cup (128g)	62	8	0	8
Dry Roasted, 1oz (28.4g)	15	2	0	2
1 Cup (128g)	68	9	0	9
Soybean Kernels				
Roasted and Toasted, 1oz (95 Kernels) (28.4g)	7	1	0	1
1 Cup Kernels (108g)	26	3	0	3

	TOTAL FAT (g)	SATURATED FAT (g)	CHOLES- TEROL (mg)	CO
panish Peanuts				
Fresh, 1oz (28g)	14	2	0	2
1 Cup (146g)	72	11	0	11
Oil-roasted, 1oz (28g)	14	2	0	2
1 Cup (147g)	72	11	0	11
Walnuts				
1oz (14 Halves) (28.4g)	18	2	0	2
1 Cup Pieces (120g)	74	7	0	7
Oats				
See also under Cereals, Porridge				
Regular, Dry				
1 Serving (27g)	2	0	0	0
1 Cup (81g)	5	1	0	1

Offal – *See under specific heading, e.g. Beef, Pork, etc.*

OIL
See also under Fat, Margarine

Almond				
1 Tbsp (13.6g)	14	1	0	1
1 Cup (218g)	218	18	0	18
Apricot Kernel				
1 Tbsp (13.6g)	14	1	0	1
1 Cup (218g)	218	14	0	14
Butter Oil (Ghee)				
1 Tbsp (12.8g)	13	8	33	10
1 Cup (205g)	204	127	525	154
Cocoa Butter				
1 Tbsp (13.6g)	14	8	0	8
1 Cup (218g)	218	130	0	131
Coconut				
1 Tbsp (13.6g)	14	12	0	12
1 Cup (218g)	218	189	0	190
Corn				
1 Tbsp (13.6g)	14	2	0	2
1 Cup (218g)	218	28	0	28
Cottonseed				
1 Tbsp (13.6g)	14	4	0	4
1 Cup (218g)	218	57	0	57
Ghee (Butter Oil)				
1 Tbsp (12.8g)	13	8	33	10
1 Cup (205g)	204	127	525	154
Grapeseed				
1 Tbsp (13.6g)	14	1	0	1
1 Cup (218g)	218	21	0	21

	TOTAL FAT (g)	SATURATED FAT (g)	CHOLES-TEROL (mg)	CQ
Hazelnut				
1 Tbsp (13.6g)	14	1	0	1
1 Cup (218g)	218	16	0	16
Olive				
1 Tbsp (13.5g)	14	2	0	2
1 Cup (216g)	216	29	0	29
Palm				
1 Tbsp (13.6g)	14	7	0	7
1 Cup (218g)	218	108	0	109
Palm Kernel				
1 Tbsp (13.6g)	14	11	0	11
1 Cup (218g)	218	178	0	179
Peanut				
1 Tbsp (13.5g)	14	2	0	2
1 Cup (216g)	216	37	0	37
Poppyseed				
1 Tbsp (13.6g)	14	2	0	2
1 Cup (218g)	218	29	0	30
Rapeseed				
1 Tbsp (13.6g)	14	1	0	1
1 Cup (218g)	218	15	0	15
Rice Bran				
1 Tbsp (13.6g)	14	3	0	3
1 Cup (218g)	218	43	0	43
Safflower				
Linoleic (over 70%), 1 Tbsp (13.6g)	14	1	0	1
1 Cup (218g)	218	20	0	20
Oleic (over 70%), 1 Tbsp (13.6g)	14	1	0	1
1 Cup (218g)	218	13	0	13
Sesame				
1 Tbsp (13.6g)	14	2	0	2
1 Cup (218g)	218	31	0	31
Soybean				
1 Tbsp (13.6g)	14	2	0	2
1 Cup (218g)	218	31	0	32
Hydrogenated, 1 Tbsp (13.6g)	14	2	0	2
1 Cup (218g)	218	33	0	33
Hydrogenated and Cottonseed, 1 Tbsp (13.6g)	14	2	0	2
1 Cup (218g)	218	39	0	40
Lecithin, 1 Tbsp (13.6g)	14	2	0	2
1 Cup (218g)	218	33	0	34
Sunflower				
Linoleic (60% and over), 1 Tbsp (13.6g)	14	1	0	1
1 Cup (218g)	218	23	0	23
Linoleic (Hydrogenated), 1 Tbsp (13.6g)	14	2	0	2
1 Cup (218g)	218	28	0	29

	TOTAL FAT (g)	SATURATED FAT (g)	CHOLES-TEROL (mg)	CQ
Walnut				
1 Tbsp (13.6g)	14	1	0	1
1 Cup (218g)	218	20	0	20
Wheat Germ				
1 Tbsp (13.6g)	14	3	0	3
1 Cup (218g)	218	41	0	41
Okra				
Boiled, 1 Cup Slices (160g)	0	0	0	0
Fresh, 1 Cup Slices (100g)	0	0	0	0
Olives				
Pickled, Tinned or Bottled, Black, 3.5oz (100g)	20	2	0	2
Pickled, Tinned or Bottled, Green, 3.5oz (100g)	13	1	0	1
Ripe, Salt-cured, Oil-coated, Greek Style, 3.5oz (100g)	36	4	0	4
Omelette				
Home Recipe, 1-Egg Omelette (64g)	15	7	301	23
Onion Rings				
Breaded, Partly fried, Frozen, Heated in Oven, 7 Rings (70g)	19	6	0	6
Onions				
Boiled, 1 Tbsp Chopped (15g)	0	0	0	0
1 Cup Chopped (210g)	0	0	0	0
Dehydrated Flakes, 1 Tbsp (5g)	0	0	0	0
¼ Cup (14g)	0	0	0	0
Fresh, 1 Tbsp Chopped (10g)	0	0	0	0
1 Cup Chopped (160g)	0	0	0	0
Shallots, Fresh, 3.5oz (100g)	0	0	0	0
Spring, Fresh, 1 Tbsp Chopped (6g)	0	0	0	0
1 Cup Chopped (100g)	0	0	0	0
Orange and Apricot Drink				
Tinned, 1 Cup (250g)	0	0	0	0
Orange and Grapefruit Juice				
Tinned, 1 Cup (247g)	0	0	0	0
Orange Drink				
Tinned, 1 Cup (246g)	0	0	0	0
From Frozen Concentrate, 1 Cup (248g)	0	0	0	0

	TOTAL FAT (g)	SATURATED FAT (g)	CHOLES- TEROL (mg)	CO
Orange Flavour Drink				
Made with Powder and Water, 1 Cup (246g)	0	0	0	0
Orange Juice				
From Non-frozen Concentrate, 1 Cup (249g)	1	0	0	0
Frozen Concentrate, Diluted, 1 Cup (249g)	0	0	0	0
Frozen Concentrate, Undiluted, 6 Fl.oz Container (213g)	0	0	0	0
Fresh, Juice from 1 Fruit (86g)	0	0	0	0
1 Cup (248g)	1	0	0	0
Tinned, 1 Cup (249g)	0	0	0	0
Orange Peel				
Candied, 1oz (28g)	0	0	0	0
Fresh, 1 Tbsp (6g)	0	0	0	0
3.5oz (100g)	0	0	0	0
Oranges				
Mandarin, Fresh, 1 Fruit (84g)	0	0	0	0
1 Cup Sections (195g)	0	0	0	0
Navels, Fresh, 1 Fruit (140g)	0	0	0	0
1 Cup Sections (165g)	0	0	0	0
Valencias, 1 Fruit (121g)	0	0	0	0
1 Cup Sections (180g)	1	0	0	0
Fresh, with Peel, 1 Fruit (159g)	1	0	0	0
1 Cup Chopped (170g)	1	0	0	0
Oyster – *See under* Fish/Shellfish				
Pancakes				
Home Recipe, 1 Cake, 6-in Diameter (73g)	5	1	39	3
1 Cake, 4-in Diameter (27g)	2	1	14	1
Made From Mix, with Egg & Milk, 1 Cake, 6-in Diameter (73g)	5	2	54	5
1 Cake, 4-in Diameter (27g)	2	1	20	2
Papayas				
Fresh, 1 Fruit (304g)	0	0	0	0
1 Cup Cubed Pieces (140g)	0	0	0	0
Parsley				
Dried, 1 Tbsp (0.4g)	0	0	0	0
¼ Cup (1.4g)	0	0	0	0
Fresh, 10 Sprigs (10g)	0	0	0	0
½ Cup Chopped (30g)	0	0	0	0

	TOTAL FAT (g)	SATURATED FAT (g)	CHOLES- TEROL (mg)	CQ
Parsnips				
Boiled, 1 Parsnip (1 Cup Slices) (160g)	1	0	0	0
Fresh, 1 Cup Slices (133g)	0	0	0	0
Passion-fruit				
Juice, 1 Cup (247g)	0	0	0	0
Fresh, 1 Fruit (18g)	0	0	0	0
Pasta – *See under* Macaroni, Spaghetti				
Pastrami				
See also under Beef				
Turkey (Spiced and Smoked), 2 Slices (56.7g)	4	1	31	3
Pastry				
Baked, made with Lard, 1 Flan Case (180g)	60	23	56	26
Baked, made with Vegetable Shortening, 1 Flan Case (180g)	60	15	0	15
Choux, 3oz (85g)	17	6	145	13
Danish, 1 Pastry (75g)	18	5	48	8
Fruit Turnover, Home Recipe, 1 Turnover (40g)	4	1	59	4
Made from Mix, made with Water, 10-oz Pack (320g)	93	23	0	23
Unbaked, made with Lard, 1 Recipe (194g)	60	23	56	26
Unbaked, made with Vegetable Shortening, 1 Recipe (194g)	60	15	0	15
Pâté de Foie Gras				
Tinned, Smoked, 1 Tbsp (13g)	6	2	20	3
1oz (28.35g)	12	4	43	6
Pâté				
Chicken Liver, Tinned, 1 Tbsp (13g)	2	1	51	3
1oz (28.35g)	4	1	111	7
Unspecified Type, 1 Tbsp (13g)	4	1	33	3
1oz (28.35g)	8	3	72	6
Peach Nectar				
Tinned, 1 Cup (249g)	0	0	0	0
Peaches				
Dried, Stewed, 1 Cup Halves (270g)	1	0	0	0
Dried, Uncooked, 1 Cup Halves (160g)	1	0	0	0
Frozen, 1 Cup Slices (250g)	0	0	0	0
Fresh, 1 Fruit (87g)	0	0	0	0
1 Cup Slices (170g)	0	0	0	0
Tinned, 1 Cup Halves or Slices (248g)	0	0	0	0

	TOTAL FAT (g)	SATURATED FAT (g)	CHOLES-TEROL (mg)	CO
Peanut Butter				
1 Tbsp (16g)	8	2	0	2
1 Cup (258g)	129	25	0	25
Peanuts				
Dried, 1oz (28.4g)	14	2	0	2
1 Cup (146g)	72	10	0	10
Boiled, 1 Cup (63g)	14	2	0	2
Dry-roasted, 1oz (28g)	14	2	0	2
1 Cup (146g)	73	10	0	10
Oil-Roasted, 1oz (28g)	14	2	0	2
1 Cup (144g)	71	10	0	10
Fresh, 1oz (28g)	14	2	0	2
1 Cup (146g)	72	10	0	10
Pear Nectar				
Tinned, 1 Cup (250g)	0	0	0	0
Pears				
Candied, 3.5oz (100g)	1	0	0	0
Dried, Stewed, 1 Cup Halves (280g)	1	0	0	0
Dried, Uncooked, 1 Cup Halves (180g)	1	0	0	0
Fresh, 1 Fruit (166g)	1	0	0	0
Tinned, 1 Cup Halves (248g)	0	0	0	0
Peas				
Edible-pod, Boiled, 1 Cup (160g)	0	0	0	0
Edible-pod, Frozen, Boiled, 1 Cup (160g)	1	0	0	0
Edible-pod, Fresh, 1 Cup (145g)	0	0	0	0
Fresh Green, Boiled, 1 Cup (160g)	0	0	0	0
Fresh Green, Fresh, 1 Cup (146g)	1	0	0	0
Green, Tinned, 1 Cup (170g)	1	0	0	0
1 Tin (313g)	1	0	0	0
Split, Boiled, 1 Cup (196g)	1	0	0	0
Split, Fresh, 1 Cup (197g)	2	0	0	0
Sprouted, Boiled, 3.5oz (100g)	1	0	0	0
Sprouted, Fresh, 1 Cup (120g)	1	0	0	0
Sweet, Wrinkled, Tinned, 1 Cup (230g)	0	0	0	0
Peas and Carrots				
Frozen, Boiled, 1 Cup (160g)	1	0	0	0
Tinned, 1 Cup (255g)	1	0	0	0
Peas and Onions				
Frozen, Boiled, 1 Cup (180g)	0	0	0	0
Tinned, 1 Cup (120g)	1	0	0	0

	TOTAL FAT (g)	SATURATED FAT (g)	CHOLES-TEROL (mg)	CQ
Peppers				
Chilli, Red, Dried Pods, 3.5oz (100g)	9	0	0	0
Chilli, Red and Green, Fresh, 1 Pepper (45g)	0	0	0	0
½ Cup Chopped (75g)	0	0	0	0
Chilli, Red and Green, Tinned, 1 Pepper (73g)	0	0	0	0
½ Cup Chopped (68g)	0	0	0	0
Chilli, Red Powder, 1 Tsp (2g)	0	0	0	0
Chilli Sauce, Green, Tinned, 1 Cup (245g)	0	0	0	0
Chilli Sauce, Red, Tinned, 1 Cup (245g)	2	0	0	0
Jalapeno, Tinned, 1 Cup Chopped (136g)	1	0	0	0
Sweet, Red and Green, Boiled, 1 Pepper (73g)	0	0	0	0
Sweet, Red and Green, Freeze-dried, 1 Tbsp (0.4g)	0	0	0	0
¼ Cup (1.6g)	0	0	0	0
Sweet, Red and Green, Fresh, 1 Pepper (74g)	0	0	0	0
Sweet, Red and Green, Tinned, 1 Cup Halves (140g)	0	0	0	0
Sweet, Stuffed with Minced Beef and Breadcrumbs 1 Pepper (185g)	10	5	70	8
Persimmons				
Japanese, Dried, 1 Fruit (34g)	0	0	0	0
Japanese, Fresh, 1 Fruit (168g)	0	0	0	0
Pheasant				
Meat and Skin, Raw, 3.5oz (100g)	5	2	98	7
½ Pheasant (400g)	37	11	284	25
Meat Only, Raw, ½ Pheasant (352g)	13	4	232	16
Breast, Meat Only, Raw, ½ Breast (182g)	6	2	106	7
Leg, Meat Only, Raw, 1 Leg (107g)	5	2	86	6
Giblets, Raw, 3.5oz (100g)	5	1	350	19
Pickles				
Cucumber, Dill, 1 Cup Slices (155g)	0	0	0	0
Cucumber, Sour, 1 Large Pickle (135g)	0	0	0	0
Cucumber, Sweet, 1 Medium Pickle (35g)	0	0	0	0
Gherkins, 1 Cup Slices (170g)	0	0	0	0
Piccalilli, with Cauliflower, Onion and Mustard, Sour 1 Cup (240g)	3	0	0	0
Piccalilli, with Cauliflower, Onion and Mustard, Sweet 1 Cup (245g)	2	0	0	0
Relish, Finely Cut or Chopped 1 Tbsp (15g)	0	0	0	0
1 Cup (245g)	2	0	0	0

	TOTAL FAT (g)	SATURATED FAT (g)	CHOLES- TEROL (mg)	CQ
PIES				
Apple				
Frozen, Baked, 1 Slice (69g)	7	2	0	2
Made with Lard, 1 Slice (118g)	13	5	13	6
Made with Vegetable Shortening, 1 Slice (118g)	13	3	0	3
Bilberry				
Made with Lard, 1 Slice (118g)	13	5	13	5
Made with Vegetable Shortening, 1 Slice (118g)	13	3	0	3
Blackberry				
Made with Lard, 1 Slice (118g)	13	5	13	6
Made with Vegetable Shortening, 1 Slice (118g)	13	3	0	3
Cherry				
Frozen, Baked, 1 Slice (73g)	9	2	0	2
Made with Lard, 1 Slice (118g)	13	5	13	6
Made with Vegetable Shortening, 1 Slice (118g)	13	4	0	4
Coconut Custard				
Frozen, Baked, 1 Slice (75g)	9	4	77	8
Made with Lard, 1 Slice (114g)	14	7	123	13
Made with Vegetable Shortening, 1 Slice (114g)	14	6	116	12
Custard				
Made with Lard, 1 Slice (114g)	13	5	123	11
Made with Vegetable Shortening, 1 Slice (114g)	13	4	120	10
Lemon Chiffon				
Made with Lard, 1 Slice (81g)	10	4	144	11
Made with Vegetable Shortening, 1 Slice (81g)	10	3	137	10
Lemon Meringue				
Made with Lard, 1 Slice (105g)	11	4	105	9
Made with Vegetable Shortening, 1 Slice (105g)	11	3	98	8
Mince				
Made with Lard, 1 Slice (118g)	14	5	13	6
Made with Vegetable Shortening, 1 Slice (118g)	14	4	1	4
Peach				
Made with Lard, 1 Slice (118g)	13	5	13	5
Made with Vegetable Shortening, 1 Slice (118g)	13	3	0	3
Pecan				
Made with Lard, 1 Slice (103g)	24	4	72	8
Made with Vegetable Shortening, 1 Slice (103g)	24	3	65	7
Pineapple				
Made with Lard, 1 Slice (118g)	13	5	13	5
Made with Vegetable Shortening, 1 Slice (118g)	13	3	0	3
Pineapple Chiffon				
Made with Lard, 1 Slice (81g)	10	4	129	10
Made with Vegetable Shortening, 1 Slice (81g)	10	3	123	9
Pineapple Custard				
Made with Lard, 1 Slice (114g)	10	4	70	7
Made with Vegetable Shortening, 1 Slice (114g)	10	3	63	6

	TOTAL FAT (g)	SATURATED FAT (g)	CHOLES- TEROL (mg)	CO
Pumpkin				
Made with Lard, 1 Slice (114g)	13	5	74	9
Made with Vegetable Shortening, 1 Slice (114g)	13	5	70	8
Raisin				
Made with Lard, 1 Slice (118g)	13	5	12	5
Made with Vegetable Shortening, 1 Slice (118g)	13	3	0	3
Rhubarb				
Made with Lard, 1 Slice (118g)	13	5	13	5
Made with Vegetable Shortening, 1 Slice (118g)	13	3	0	3
Strawberry				
Made with Lard, 1 Slice (93g)	7	3	7	3
Made with Vegetable Shortening, 1 Slice (93g)	7	2	0	2
Sweet Potato				
Made with Lard, 1 Slice (114g)	13	6	68	9
Made with Vegetable Shortening, 1 Slice (114g)	13	5	62	8
Pigeon				
Meat and Skin, Raw, 1 Pigeon (199g)	47	17	189	26
Meat Only, Raw, 1 Pigeon (168g)	13	3	151	11
Breast Meat Only, Raw, 1 Breast (101g)	5	1	91	6
Giblets, Raw, 3.5oz (100g)	7	2	350	20
Pimientos				
Tinned or Bottled, 4oz Tin or Jar (113g)	1	0	0	0
Pineapple				
Candied, 8oz Container (227g)	1	0	0	0
Fresh, 1 Slice (84g)	0	0	0	0
1 Cup Pieces (155g)	1	0	0	0
Frozen, Chunks, 1 Cup Chunks (245g)	0	0	0	0
Tinned, 1 Cup Chunks (250g)	0	0	0	0
Pineapple Juice				
Frozen Concentrate, Diluted, 1 Cup (250g)	0	0	0	0
Frozen Concentrate, Undiluted, 6 Fl.oz Container (216g)	0	0	0	0
Tinned, 1 Cup (250g)	0	0	0	0
Pineapple and Grapefruit Juice				
Tinned, 1 Cup (250g)	0	0	0	0
Pineapple and Orange Juice				
Tinned, 1 Cup (250g)	0	0	0	0
Pistachio Nut				
Dried, 1oz (47 Kernels) (28.4g)	14	2	0	2
1 Cup (128g)	62	8	0	8

	TOTAL FAT (g)	SATURATED FAT (g)	CHOLES- TEROL (mg)	CO
Pizza				
Cheese Topping, Baked from Home Recipe, 1 Slice (65g)	5	2	12	3
Cheese Topping, Chilled, Baked, 1 Slice (60g)	4	1	11	2
Cheese Topping, Frozen, Baked, 1 Slice (57g)	4	2	10	2
Cheese Topping, Frozen, Baked, 1 Pizza (425g)	28	10	55	13
4 Mini-pizzas (312g)	21	7	41	9
Cheese, Ham and Vegetable Topping, Baked, 1 Slice (65g)	4	1	17	2
Pepperoni and Cheese Topping, Baked, 1 Slice (53g)	5	2	11	2
Sausage Topping, No Cheese, Baked from Home Recipe 1 Slice (67g)	6	2	13	2
Sausage Topping, with Cheese, Baked from Home Recipe 1 Slice (67g)	9	2	19	3
Plantain				
Boiled or Stewed, 1 Cup Slices (154g)	0	0	0	0
Fresh, 1 Cup Slices (148g)	1	0	0	0
Ploughman's Lunch (Cheddar, French Bread, Butter and Pickle)				
Made with 4oz (115g) Cheddar, 3 Pats Butter	52	32	153	40
Plums				
Fresh, 1 Fruit (66g)	0	0	0	0
Tinned, 1 Cup (252g)	0	0	0	0
Poached Egg				
1 Large Egg (50g)	6	2	273	15
Pomegranate				
Fresh, 1 Fruit (154g)	1	0	0	0
Popcorn				
Plain, 1 Cup (6g)	0	0	0	0
Sugar Coated, 1 Cup (35g)	1	0	0	0
With Butter and Salt Added, 1 Cup (9g)	2	1	4	1
With Coconut Oil and Salt Added, 1 Cup (9g)	2	1	0	1

PORK

See also under Luncheon Meat

Backfat				
Raw, 1 lb (453.6g)	402	146	259	160

	TOTAL FAT (g)	SATURATED FAT (g)	CHOLES- TEROL (mg)	CQ
Bacon				
Cured, Tinned, 3.5oz (100g)	72	23	89	28
Long Back, Grilled, 2 Slices (46.5g)	4	1	27	3
Long Back, Raw, 2 Slices (56.7g)	4	1	28	3
Streaky, Grilled, Shallow-fried or Roasted,				
3 Medium Slices (19g)	9	3	16	4
Streaky, Raw, 3 Medium Slices (68g)	39	15	46	17
Top Back, Grilled or Roasted, 3 Slices (34g)	13	4	36	6
Top Back, Raw, 3 Slices (68g)	25	9	47	11
Belly of Pork				
Raw, 1 lb (453.6g)	241	88	327	105
Blade				
Boneless, Lean and Fat, Roasted, 3oz (85g)	20	7	57	10
Boneless, Lean and Fat, Raw, 4oz (113g)	25	9	60	12
Brawn				
Cured, 1 Slice or 1oz (28.35g)	5	1	23	3
Brains				
Braised, 3oz (85g)	8	2	2169	110
Raw, 4oz (113g)	10	2	2480	126
Bratwurst				
Cooked, 1 Link (85g)	22	8	51	11
Composite Cuts				
Lean and Fat, Raw, 1 lb (453.6g)	102	37	327	54
Lean Only, Roasted, 3oz (85g)	11	4	79	8
Lean Only, Raw, 1 lb (453.6g)	31	11	295	25
Ears				
Simmered, 1 Ear (111g)	12	4	100	9
Raw, 1 Ear (113g)	17	6	93	11
Fat				
Cooked, 1oz (28.35g)	21	8	26	9
3.5oz (100g)	75	27	91	32
Raw, 1oz (28.35g)	22	8	26	9
3.5oz (100g)	77	28	93	33
Gammon Steak				
Boneless, Extra Lean, 1 Slice (56.7g)	2	1	26	2
Gorge				
Raw, 4oz (113g)	79	29	102	34

	TOTAL FAT (g)	SATURATED FAT (g)	CHOLES-TEROL (mg)	CQ
Ham				
See also under Ham				
Boneless				
Extra Lean (5% Fat), Roasted, 3oz (85g)	5	2	45	4
Extra Lean (5% Fat), Unheated, 4oz (113g)	6	2	52	4
Regular (11% Fat), Roasted, 3oz (85g)	8	3	50	5
Regular (11% Fat), Unheated, 4oz (113g)	12	4	64	7
Centre Slice				
Lean and Fat, Unheated, 4oz (113g)	15	5	61	8
Lean Only, Raw, 4oz (113g)	9	3	79	7
Croquette				
1 Croquette (65g)	10	4	46	6
Cured				
Chopped, 1 Slice (28.35g)	5	2	14	2
Dry, Long Cure, Lean, 3.5oz (100g)	25	9	62	12
Minced, 1 Slice (28.35g)	6	2	20	3
Devilled Ham				
Tinned, 4½oz Tin (128g)	41	15	83	19
1 Cup (225g)	73	26	146	34
Patties				
Grilled, 1 Patty (59.5g)	18	7	43	9
Unheated, 1 Patty (65.2g)	18	7	46	9
Tinned				
Extra Lean (4% Fat), Roasted, 3oz (85g)	4	1	26	3
Extra Lean (4% Fat), Unheated, 4oz (113g)	5	2	44	4
Regular (13% Fat), Roasted, 3oz (85g)	13	4	53	7
Regular (13% Fat), Unheated, 4oz (113g)	15	5	44	7
Whole				
Lean and Fat, Roasted, 3oz (85g)	14	5	53	8
Lean and Fat, Unheated, 4oz (113g)	21	8	64	11
Lean Only, Unheated, 4oz (113g)	6	2	60	5
Heart				
Braised, 1 Heart (129g)	7	2	285	16
Raw, 1 Heart (226g)	10	3	296	17
Jowl				
Raw, 4oz (113g)	79	29	102	34
Kidneys				
Braised, 3oz (85g)	4	1	408	22
Raw, 1 Kidney (233g)	8	2	743	40
Lard				
1 Tbsp (12.8g)	13	5	12	6
1 Cup (205g)	205	80	195	91

	TOTAL FAT (g)	SATURATED FAT (g)	CHOLES- TEROL (mg)	CO
Leaf Fat				
Raw, 1oz (28.35g)	27	13	31	15
4oz (113g)	106	51	124	58
Leg				
Fillet End				
Lean and Fat, Roasted, 3oz (85g)	15	5	81	10
Lean and Fat, Raw, 1 lb (453.6g)	79	28	299	44
Lean Only, Roasted, 3oz (85g)	9	3	82	7
Lean Only, Raw, 1 lb (453.6g)	24	8	277	22
Knuckle End				
Lean and Fat, Roasted, 3oz (85g)	19	7	78	11
Lean and Fat, Raw, 1 lb (453.6g)	106	38	308	54
Lean Only, Roasted, 3oz (85g)	9	3	78	7
Lean Only, Raw, 1 lb (453.6g)	26	9	272	23
Whole				
Lean and Fat, Roasted, 3oz (85g)	18	6	79	10
Lean and Fat, Raw, 1 lb (453.6g)	94	34	336	51
Lean Only, Roasted, 3oz (85g)	9	3	80	7
Lean Only, Raw, 1 lb (453.6g)	25	9	308	24
Liver				
Braised, 3oz (85g)	4	1	302	16
Cured, 1 Slice (28.35g)	7	3	49	5
Fried, 3oz Slice (85g)	10	3	372	22
Raw, 4oz (113g)	4	1	340	18
Luncheon Meat				
Cured, Tinned, 1 Slice (28.35g)	9	3	18	4
Loin Chops				
Blade				
Lean and Fat, Braised, 1 Chop (67g)	23	8	72	12
Lean and Fat, Grilled, 1 Chop (77g)	26	9	76	13
Lean and Fat, Roasted, 1 Chop (88g)	27	10	79	14
Lean and Fat, Shallow-fried, 1 Chop (89g)	33	12	85	16
Lean and Fat, Raw, 1 Chop (110g)	31	11	79	15
1 lb (453.6g)	130	47	327	63
Lean Only, Braised, 1 Chop (50g)	10	4	57	6
Lean Only, Grilled, 1 Chop (59g)	13	4	59	7
Lean Only, Roasted, 1 Chop (71g)	14	5	63	8
Lean Only, Shallow-fried, 1 Chop (62g)	12	4	60	7
Lean Only, Raw, 1 Chop (82g)	9	3	53	6
1 lb (453.6g)	50	17	290	32
Centre Loin				
Lean and Fat, Braised, 1 Chop (75g)	19	7	80	11
Lean and Fat, Grilled, 1 Chop (87g)	19	7	84	11

	TOTAL FAT (g)	SATURATED FAT (g)	CHOLES- TEROL (mg)	CQ
Lean and Fat, Roasted, 1 Chop (88g)	19	7	80	11
Lean and Fat, Shallow-fried, 1 Chop (89g)	27	10	92	14
Lean and Fat, Raw, 1 Chop (124g)	27	10	87	14
1 lb (453.6g)	99	36	318	52
Lean Only, Braised, 1 Chop (61g)	8	3	68	6
Lean only, Grilled, 1 Chop (72g)	8	3	71	6
Lean Only, Roasted, 1 Chop (75g)	10	3	68	7
Lean Only, Shallow-fried, 1 Chop (67g)	11	4	72	7
Lean Only, Raw, 1 Chop (98g)	7	2	62	6
1 lb (453.6g)	32	11	286	26
Fore Loin				
Lean and Fat, Braised, 1 Chop (67g)	18	7	64	10
Lean and Fat, Grilled, 1 Chop (77g)	20	7	72	11
Lean and Fat, Roasted, 1 Chop (79g)	19	7	64	10
Lean and Fat, Shallow-fried, 1 Chop (88g)	29	11	74	14
Lean and Fat, Raw, 1 Chop (112g)	26	10	72	13
1 lb (453.6g)	106	38	290	53
Lean Only, Braised, 1 Chop (53g)	8	3	51	5
Lean Only, Grilled, 1 Chop (63g)	9	3	59	6
Lean Only, Roasted, 1 Chop (66g)	9	3	52	6
Lean Only, Shallow-fried, 1 Chop (62g)	10	3	50	6
Lean Only, Raw, 1 Chop (86g)	7	2	47	5
1 lb (453.6g)	34	12	250	24
Hind Loin				
Lean and Fat, Braised, 1 Chop (71g)	18	7	75	10
Lean and Fat, Grilled, 1 Chop (84g)	21	8	82	12
Lean and Fat, Roasted, 1 Chop (84g)	17	6	76	10
Lean and Fat, Raw, 1 Chop (119g)	27	10	83	14
1 lb (453.6g)	101	37	318	53
Lean Only, Braised, 1 Chop (57g)	7	3	63	6
Lean Only, Grilled, 1 Chop (68g)	9	3	67	7
Lean Only, Roasted, 1 Chop (74g)	10	3	67	7
Lean Only, Raw, 1 Chop (92g)	6	2	58	5
1 lb (453.6g)	31	11	286	25
Tenderloin				
Lean Only, Roasted, 3oz (85g)	4	1	79	5
Lean Only, Raw, 4oz (113g)	3	1	72	5
Top Loin				
Lean and Fat, Braised, 1 Chop (70g)	20	7	67	11
Lean and Fat, Grilled, 1 Chop (82g)	24	9	76	12
Lean and Fat, Roasted, 1 Chop (83g)	21	8	68	11
Lean and Fat, Shallow-fried, 1 Chop (86g)	29	10	72	14
Lean and Fat, Raw, 1 Chop (118g)	30	11	77	15
1 lb (453.6g)	116	42	295	57
Lean Only, Braised, 1 Chop (53g)	8	3	51	5
Lean Only, Grilled, 1 Chop (64g)	10	3	60	6
Lean Only, Roasted, 1 Chop (68g)	9	3	54	6

	TOTAL FAT (g)	SATURATED FAT (g)	CHOLES- TEROL (mg)	CQ
Lean Only, Shallow-fried, 1 Chop (61g)	9	3	49	6
Lean Only, Raw, 1 Chop (88g)	7	2	48	5
1 lb (453.6g)	34	12	250	24
Whole Loin				
Lean and Fat, Braised, 1 Chop (71g)	20	7	72	11
Lean and Fat, Grilled, 1 Chop (82g)	22	8	77	12
Lean and Fat, Roasted, 1 Chop (82g)	20	7	74	11
Lean and Fat, Raw, 1 Chop (119g)	29	10	81	15
1 lb (453.6g)	110	40	308	55
Lean Only, Braised, 1 Chop (55g)	8	3	58	6
Lean Only, Grilled, 1 Chop (66g)	10	4	63	7
Lean Only, Roasted, 1 Chop (69g)	10	3	62	6
Lean Only, Raw, 1 Chop (91g)	7	2	55	5
1 lb (453.6g)	34	12	272	26
Lungs				
Braised, 3oz (85g)	3	1	329	17
Raw, 3.46oz (98g)	3	1	314	17
Pancreas				
Braised, 3oz (85g)	9	3	268	17
Raw, 4oz (113g)	15	5	218	16
Pork Pie				
¼ Medium Pie (170g)	72	27	206	37
Pork Pie Filling				
Raw, 8oz (227g)	60	22	175	31
Pork Scratchings				
Simmered, 3oz (85g)	24	9	122	15
Raw, 1oz (28.35g)	7	2	45	5
Salami				
Dry or Hard, 1 Slice (10g)	3	1	8	2
1 Package, Net Weight 4oz (113g)	38	13	89	18
Salt Pork				
Raw, 8oz (227g)	183	67	195	77
Sausages				
See also under Sausages				
Bratwurst				
Cooked, 1 Link (85g)	22	8	51	11
Brawn				
Cured, 1 Slice or 1oz (28.35g)	5	1	23	3

	TOTAL FAT (g)	SATURATED FAT (g)	CHOLES- TEROL (mg)	CO
Italian Sausage				
Grilled, 1 Link (67g)	17	6	52	9
1 Link (83g)	21	8	65	11
Raw, 1 Link (91g)	29	10	69	14
1 Link (113g)	35	13	86	17
Liver Sausage				
1 Slice (28.35g)	8	3	45	5
Polish Sausage				
1oz (28.35g)	8	3	20	4
1 Sausage (227g)	65	23	159	32
Salami				
Dry or Hard, 1 Slice (10g)	3	1	8	2
1 Package, Net Weight 4oz (113g)	38	13	89	18
Sausage Meat				
Cooked, 1 Patty (27g)	8	3	22	4
1 Link (13g)	4	1	11	2
Raw, 1 Patty (57g)	23	8	39	10
1 Link (28g)	11	4	19	5
Sausage Roll				
1 Sausage Roll (55g)	18	7	17	8
Sausages				
Tinned, Drained Solids, 1 Sausage (12g)	4	1	11	2
Tinned, Solids and Liquid, 8oz Tin (approx. 16				
Sausages) (227g)	87	31	152	39
Smoked Link Sausage				
Grilled, 1 Link (68g)	22	8	46	10
1 Little Link (16g)	5	2	11	2

Shoulder

	TOTAL FAT (g)	SATURATED FAT (g)	CHOLES- TEROL (mg)	CO
Arm Picnic				
Lean and Fat, Roasted, 3oz (85g)	18	7	49	9
Lean Only, Roasted, 3oz (85g)	6	2	41	4
Blade				
Lean and Fat, Braised, 1 Steak (160g)	46	17	178	26
Lean and Fat, Grilled, 1 Steak (185g)	53	19	191	29
Lean and Fat, Roasted, 1 Steak (185g)	47	17	180	26
Lean and Fat, Raw, 1 Steak (264g)	62	22	193	32
1 lb (453.6g)	106	38	331	55
Lean Only, Braised, 1 Steak (130g)	23	8	151	15
Lean Only, Grilled, 1 Steak (151g)	28	10	159	18
Lean Only, Roasted, 1 Steak (158g)	27	9	155	17
Lean Only, Raw, 1 Steak (210g)	20	7	143	14
1 lb (453.6g)	42	15	308	30
Picnic Shoulder				
Lean and Fat, Braised, 3oz (85g)	22	8	93	13
Lean and Fat, Roasted, 3oz (85g)	22	8	80	12
Lean and Fat, Raw, 1 lb (453.6g)	101	36	327	53

	TOTAL FAT (g)	SATURATED FAT (g)	CHOLES-TEROL (mg)	CQ
Lean Only, Braised, 3oz (85g)	10	4	97	8
Lean Only, Roasted, 3oz (85g)	11	4	81	8
Lean Only, Raw, 1 lb (453.6g)	28	10	295	25
Whole				
Lean and Fat, Roasted, 3oz (85g)	22	8	82	12
Lean and Fat, Raw, 1 lb (453.6g)	104	37	327	54
Lean Only, Roasted, 3oz (85g)	13	4	83	9
Lean Only, Raw, 1 lb (453.6g)	36	12	304	28
Spareribs				
Lean and Fat, Braised, 3oz (85g)	26	10	103	15
Lean and Fat, Raw, 1 lb (453.6g)	107	42	354	60
In Barbecue Sauce, 1 Serving (350g)	35	12	121	19
Spleen				
Braised, 3oz (85g)	3	1	428	22
Raw, 4oz (113g)	3	1	410	21
Stomach				
Raw, 4oz (113g)	11	4	218	15
Tail				
Simmered, 3oz (85g)	30	11	110	16
Raw, 4oz (113g)	38	13	110	19
Tongue				
Braised, 3oz (85g)	16	6	124	12
Raw, 4oz (113g)	19	7	114	13
Trotters				
Pickled, 3oz (100g)	16	6	92	10
1 lb (453.6g)	73	25	417	46
Simmered, ½ Trotter (71g)	9	3	71	7
Raw, ½ Trotter (95g)	18	6	101	11
Porridge				
Made with ½ Milk, ½ Water, 1 Serving (235g)	5	1	3	1
Made with Skimmed Milk, 1 Serving (235g)	6	1	6	2
Made with Water, 1 Serving (235g)	5	1	0	1
Made with Whole Milk, 1 Serving (235g)	17	9	50	11
Potato Crisps				
1oz Packet (28.4g)	10	3	0	3
Potato Pancakes				
Home-prepared, 1 Pancake (76g)	13	3	94	8

	TOTAL FAT (g)	SATURATED FAT (g)	CHOLES-TEROL (mg)	CQ
Potato Salad				
1 Cup (250g)	21	4	170	12
Potato Sticks				
1oz Packet (28.4g)	10	3	0	3

POTATOES

	TOTAL FAT (g)	SATURATED FAT (g)	CHOLES-TEROL (mg)	CQ
Au Gratin				
Home-prepared using Butter, 1 Cup (245g)	19	12	56	15
Home-prepared using Margarine, 1 Cup (245g)	19	9	37	11
Baked				
Flesh, 1 Medium Potato (156g)	0	0	0	0
Flesh and Skin, 1 Medium Potato (202g)	0	0	0	0
Skin 1 Potato (58g)	0	0	0	0
With Baked Beans, 1 Medium with ½ Tin (220g) Baked Beans	1	0	0	0
With Butter, 1 Medium with 1 Pat Butter	4	3	11	3
With Cottage Cheese, 1 Medium with ½ Cup Low-fat Cottage Cheese	2	1	10	2
With Grated Cheese, 1 Medium with 1 Pat Butter, 55g Cheddar	23	15	71	18
With Soured Cream and Chives, 1 Medium Potato with 2 Tbsp Soured Cream (302g)	22	10	23	11
Boiled				
Skin and Flesh, 1 Medium Potato (136g)	0	0	0	0
Chips				
See also under Chips				
Frozen, Heated in Oven, 1 Cup (50g)	9	4	0	4
Frozen, Fried in Animal Fat and Vegetable Oil, 1 Cup (57g)	9	4	7	4
Frozen, Fried in Vegetable Oil, 1 Cup (57g)	9	3	0	3
Crisps				
1oz Packet (28.4g)	10	3	0	3
Hashed Brown				
Frozen, Plain, 3.5oz (100g)	12	4	3	5
Frozen, with Butter Sauce, 3.5oz (100g)	9	3	23	5
Home Recipe, 1 Cup (156g)	22	9	0	9
Mashed				
Dehydrated Flakes without Milk, Dry Form, 1 Cup (200g)	1	0	0	0
Dehydrated Flakes without Milk, made with Whole Milk and Butter, 1 Cup (210g)	12	7	29	9
Dehydrated Flakes, without Milk, made with Whole Milk and Margarine, 1 Cup (210g)	12	3	8	4
Dehydrated Flakes with Milk, Dry Form, 1 Cup (200g)	2	1	4	1

	TOTAL FAT (g)	SATURATED FAT (g)	CHOLES-TEROL (mg)	CQ
Dehydrated Flakes with Milk, made with Water and Margarine, 1 Cup (210g)	5	1	4	2
Home Recipe, made with Whole Milk, 1 Cup (210g)	1	1	4	1
Home Recipe, made with Whole Milk and Butter, 1 Cup (210g)	9	6	25	7
Home Recipe, made with Whole Milk and Margarine, 1 Cup (210g)	9	2	4	2
Microwaved				
Flesh Only, 1 Medium Potato (156g)	0	0	0	0
Flesh and Skin, 1 Medium Potato (202g)	0	0	0	0
Skin from 1 Potato (58g)	0	0	0	0
O'Brien (milk, onions, peppers, bread crumbs, butter)				
Frozen, Prepared, 3.5oz (100g)	13	3	23	4
Home Recipe, 1 Cup (194g)	3	2	8	2
Salad				
1 Cup (285g)	17	3	171	12
Scalloped				
Home Recipe, made with Butter, 1 Cup (245g)	9	6	29	7
Home Recipe, made with Margarine, 1 Cup (245g)	9	3	15	4
Tinned				
Drained Solids, 1 Cup (180g)	0	0	0	0
Solids and Liquid, 1 Cup Whole (300g)	1	0	0	0
1 Tin (454g)	1	0	0	0
Uncooked				
Flesh, 1 Medium Potato (112g)	0	0	0	0
Skin from 1 Potato (38g)	0	0	0	0
Potted Meat				
Variety of Meats, 5.5oz Tin (156g)	30	14	122	20
1 Cup (225g)	43	20	176	29
Poultry – *See under specific name of bird*				
Pretzels				
1 Pretzel (16g)	1	0	0	0
1 Cup (106g)	5	1	0	1
Prickly Pear				
Fresh, 1 Fruit (103g)	1	0	0	0
Prune Juice				
Tinned, 1 Cup (256g)	0	0	0	0
Prunes				
Dried, Stewed, 1 Cup, without Pits (238g)	1	0	0	0

	TOTAL FAT (g)	SATURATED FAT (g)	CHOLES- TEROL (mg)	CQ
Dried, Uncooked, 1 Cup, without Pits (161g)	1	0	0	0
Tinned, 1 Cup (234g)	1	0	0	0

PUDDINGS

	TOTAL FAT (g)	SATURATED FAT (g)	CHOLES- TEROL (mg)	CQ
Blancmange				
Home Recipe, 1 Cup (255g)	10	6	36	7
Bread and Butter Pudding				
1 Serving (170g)	29	7	170	15
Bread Pudding				
With Raisins, 1 Cup (265g)	16	8	180	17
Chocolate Pudding				
With Milk and Starch Base Mix, Cooked, 1 Cup (260g)	8	4	31	6
Home Recipe, 1 Cup (260g)	12	7	29	8
Christmas Pudding				
1 Serving (170g)	81	9	102	14
Cream Pudding				
1 Cup (165g)	8	4	160	12
Custard Dessert				
Made with Milk and Vegetable-gum Base Mix, Cooked, 3.5oz (100g)	4	2	12	3
Instant Pudding				
Made with Milk and Starch Base Mix, without Cooking, 1 Cup (260g)	7	4	29	5
Rice Pudding				
With Raisins, 1 Cup (265g)	8	5	29	6
Sponge Pudding				
1 Serving (115g)	19	7	92	11
Suet Pudding				
1 Serving (85g)	15	9	3	9
Tapioca Dessert				
1 Cup (165g)	8	4	160	12
Trifle				
1 Serving (285g)	17	8	143	15
Turnover				
Home Recipe, 1 Turnover (40g)	4	1	59	4
Vanilla Pudding				
Home Recipe, 1 Cup (255g)	10	6	36	7
Pumpkin				
Boiled, 1 Cup Mashed (245g)	0	0	0	0
Fresh, 1 Cup, 1-in Cubes (116g)	0	0	0	0
Tinned, 1 Cup (245g)	1	0	0	0
Flowers, Boiled, 1 Cup (134g)	0	0	0	0
Flowers, Fresh, 1 Cup (33g)	0	0	0	0

	TOTAL FAT (g)	SATURATED FAT (g)	CHOLES- TEROL (mg)	CO
Purslane				
Boiled, 1 Cup (115g)	0	0	0	0
Fresh, 1 Cup (43g)	0	0	0	0
Quail				
Meat and Skin, Raw, 1 Quail (109g)	13	4	83	8
Meat Only, Raw, 1 Quail (92g)	4	1	64	4
Breast, Meat Only, Raw, 1 Breast (56g)	2	1	33	2
Giblets, Raw, 3.5oz (100g)	6	2	350	20
Quiche Lorraine				
Home Recipe, 1 Slice (115g)	32	14	150	22
Quince				
Fresh, 1 Fruit (92g)	0	0	0	0
Rabbit				
Domesticated, Flesh Only, Stewed, 1 Cup Chopped (140g)	14	6	127	12
Domesticated, Flesh Only, Raw, 3.5oz (100g)	8	3	65	6
Wild, Flesh Only, Raw, 3.5oz (100g)	5	2	65	5
Radish Seeds				
Sprouted, Fresh, 1 Cup (38g)	1	0	0	0
Radishes				
Oriental, Boiled, 1 Cup Slices (147g)	0	0	0	0
Oriental, Dried, 1 Cup (116g)	1	0	0	0
Oriental, Fresh, 1 Radish, 7-in Long (338g)	0	0	0	0
Fresh, 10 Radishes (45g)	0	0	0	0
White Icicle, Fresh, 1 Radish (100g)	0	0	0	0
Raisins				
Golden Seedless, 1 Cup Packed (165g)	1	0	0	0
Seeded, 1 Cup Packed (165g)	1	0	0	0
Seedless, 1 Cup Packed (165g)	1	0	0	0
Raspberries				
Frozen, 1 Cup (250g)	0	0	0	0
Fresh, 1 Cup (123g)	1	0	0	0
Tinned, 1 Cup (256g)	0	0	0	0
Rhubarb				
Cooked, 1 Cup (240g)	0	0	0	0

	TOTAL FAT (g)	SATURATED FAT (g)	CHOLES- TEROL (mg)	CQ
RICE				
Basmati				
Cooked, 1 Cup, Hot (175g)	0	0	0	0
Bran				
3.5oz (100g)	16	3	0	3
Bran Polish				
1 Cup (105g)	13	2	0	2
Brown				
Cooked, 1 Cup, Hot (195g)	1	0	0	0
Raw, 1 Cup (185g)	4	0	0	0
Rice Pudding				
With Raisins, 1 Cup (265g)	8	5	29	6
White				
Glutinous, (Mochi Gomi), Uncooked, 3.5oz (100g)	1	0	0	0
Polished, Cooked, 1 Cup, Hot (205g)	0	0	0	0
Polished, Uncooked, 1 Cup (185g)	1	0	0	0
Pre-cooked Instant, Dry, 1 Cup (95g)	0	0	0	0
Wild				
Uncooked, 1 Cup (160g)	1	0	0	0
Roast Beef				
Home Recipe, 1 Portion	26	11	72	14
Roast Chicken				
Home Recipe, 1 Portion (235g)	31	9	221	20
Roast Leg of Lamb				
Home Recipe, 3.5oz (100g)	24	13	98	18
Roast Shoulder of Lamb				
Home Recipe, 3.5oz (100g)	32	18	98	23
Rock Cakes				
1 Cake (55g)	9	3	22	4
Rolls – *See under* Bread				
Roselle				
Fresh, 1 Cup (57g)	0	0	0	0
Rusk				
Hard Crisp Bread or Toast, 1 Rusk (9g)	1	0	1	0
13 Rusks (113g)	10	3	10	3
Rye				
Whole-grain, 3.5oz (100g)	2	0	0	0

	TOTAL FAT (g)	SATURATED FAT (g)	CHOLES-TEROL (mg)	CQ

SALAD DRESSINGS

Blue Cheese Dressing

	TOTAL FAT (g)	SATURATED FAT (g)	CHOLES-TEROL (mg)	CQ
Low-fat, 1 Calorie/tsp, 1 Tbsp (15g)	0	0	0	0
1 Cup (245g)	3	3	0	2
Low-fat, 5 Calorie/tsp, 1 Tbsp (16g)	1	1	0	1
1 Cup (255g)	15	8	0	8
Regular, 3.5oz (100g)	52	10	17	11
French Dressing				
Commercial, Regular, 1 Tbsp (15.6g)	6	2	9	2
1 Cup (250g)	103	24	145	31
Low-fat, 1 Calorie/tsp, 3.5oz (100g)	0	0	0	0
Low-fat, 5 Calorie/tsp, 1 Tbsp (16.3g)	1	0	1	0
1 Cup (260g)	15	2	16	3
Home Recipe, 1 Tbsp (14.0g)	10	2	0	2
1 Cup (220g)	154	28	0	28
Italian Dressing				
Low-fat, 2 Calories/tsp, 1 Tbsp (15.0g)	2	0	1	0
1 Cup (240g)	24	3	14	4
Regular, 1 Tbsp (14.7g)	7	1	0	1
1 Cup (235g)	114	17	0	17
Mayonnaise				
Imitation, made with Milk Cream, 1 Tbsp (15.0g)	1	0	7	1
1 Cup (240g)	12	7	103	12
Imitation, made with Egg and Soybean Oil,				
1 Tbsp (15.0g)	3	1	4	1
1 Cup (240g)	46	8	58	11
Imitation, made without Egg or Milk, made with				
Soybean Oil, 1 Tbsp (14.0g)	7	1	0	1
1 Cup (225g)	107	17	0	17
Made with Egg and Soybean and Safflower Oil,				
1 Tbsp (13.8g)	11	1	8	2
1 Cup (220g)	175	19	130	26
Made with Egg and Soybean Oil, 1 Tbsp (13.8g)	11	2	8	2
1 Cup (220g)	175	26	130	33
Roquefort Dressing				
Low-fat, 1 Calorie/tsp, 1 Tbsp (15g)	0	0	0	0
1 Cup (245g)	3	3	0	2
Low-fat, 5 Calorie/tsp, 1 Tbsp (16g)	1	1	0	1
1 Cup (255g)	15	8	0	8
Regular, 3.5oz (100g)	52	10	17	11
Russian Dressing				
Low-cal, 1 Tbsp (16.3g)	1	0	1	0
1 Cup (260g)	10	2	16	2
Regular, 1 Tbsp (15.3g)	8	1	3	1
1 Cup (245g)	125	18	44	20

Salad Cream

	TOTAL FAT (g)	SATURATED FAT (g)	CHOLES-TEROL (mg)	CQ
Low-cal, 8 Calories/tsp, 1 Tbsp (16g)	2	0	8	1
1 Cup (250g)	32	6	125	12
Regular, 1 Tbsp (15g)	6	1	8	2
1 Cup (235g)	99	18	118	24
Sesame Seed Dressing				
1 Tbsp (15.3g)	7	1	0	1
1 Cup (245g)	111	15	0	15
Thousand Island Dressing				
Low-cal, 10 Calories/tsp, 1 Tbsp (15.3g)	2	0	2	0
1 Cup (245g)	26	4	37	6
Regular, 1 Tbsp (15.6g)	6	1	4	1
1 Cup (250g)	89	15	65	18
Vinaigrette				
Home Recipe, 1 Tbsp (15.6g)	8	1	0	1
1 Cup (250g)	125	23	0	23

SALADS

	TOTAL FAT (g)	SATURATED FAT (g)	CHOLES-TEROL (mg)	CQ
Chef's Salad (Mixed Vegetables with Turkey, Ham and Cheese, without Dressing)				
1½ Cups (326g)	16	8	139	15
Coleslaw				
1 Cup (138g)	15	2	7	2
Fruit Salad				
1 Cup (249g)	0	0	0	0
Lobster Salad				
½ Cup (260g)	17	3	120	9
Mixed Salad				
Without Dressing, 1½ Cups (207g)	0	0	0	0
With Cheese and Egg, without Dressing, 1½ Cups (217g)	6	3	98	8
With Chicken, without Dressing, 1½ Cups (218g)	2	1	72	4
With Pasta and Seafood, without Dressing, 1½ Cups (417g)	21	3	50	5
With Shrimp, without Dressing, 1½ Cups (236g)	2	1	180	10
Potato Salad				
1 Cup (285g)	17	3	171	12
Tuna Salad				
3oz (85g)	8	1	11	2
1 Cup (205g)	19	3	27	5

	TOTAL FAT (g)	SATURATED FAT (g)	CHOLES-TEROL (mg)	CQ
Salami				
Bierwurst, 1 Slice (23g)	7	3	14	4
Pork, 1 Slice (10g)	3	1	8	2
Smoked, 1 Slice (28.35g)	6	3	18	3
Turkey, Cooked, 1 Slice (28.4g)	4	1	23	2

	TOTAL FAT (g)	SATURATED FAT (g)	CHOLES-TEROL (mg)	CQ
Salsify				
Boiled, 1 Cup Slices (135g)	0	0	0	0
Fresh, 1 Cup Slices (133g)	0	0	0	0
Salt				
Table, 1 Tsp (5.5g)	0	0	0	0
Sandwich Spread				
Pork and Beef, 1 Tbsp (15g)	3	1	6	1
1oz (28.35g)	5	2	11	2
With Chopped Pickle, Unspecified Oils, 1 Tbsp (15.3g)	5	1	12	1
1 Cup (245g)	83	13	186	22

SANDWICHES
See also under Bread

	TOTAL FAT (g)	SATURATED FAT (g)	CHOLES-TEROL (mg)	CQ
Bacon				
1 Sandwich (74g)	15	6	28	7
BLT (Bacon, Lettuce and Tomato)				
1 Sandwich (100g)	23	9	50	12
Cheese and Tomato				
1 Sandwich (100g)	25	15	71	19
Chicken, Plain				
1 Sandwich (182g)	29	9	60	12
Chicken and Cheese				
1 Sandwich (228g)	39	12	76	16
Egg and Cheese				
1 Sandwich (156g)	19	7	291	21
Egg Salad				
1 Sandwich (153g)	24	8	264	21
Fish				
With Tartar Sauce, 1 Sandwich (158g)	23	5	55	8
With Tartar Sauce and Cheese, 1 Sandwich (183g)	29	8	68	12
Ham				
1 Sandwich (113g)	12	5	43	7
Ham and Cheese				
1 Sandwich (146g)	15	6	58	9
Ham, Egg and Cheese				
1 Sandwich (143g)	16	7	245	20
Ploughman's Lunch (Cheese, French Bread, Butter and Pickle)				
Made with 4oz (115g) Cheddar, 3 Pats Butter	52	32	153	40
Roast Beef, Plain				
1 Sandwich (139g)	14	4	52	6

	TOTAL FAT (g)	SATURATED FAT (g)	CHOLES- TEROL (mg)	CQ
Roast Beef and Cheese				
1 Sandwich (176g)	18	9	77	13
Tuna				
1 Regular	13	4	26	6
Sapodilla				
Fresh, 1 Fruit (170g)	2	0	0	0

SAUCES

	TOTAL FAT (g)	SATURATED FAT (g)	CHOLES- TEROL (mg)	CQ
Barbecue				
1 Cup (250g)	5	1	0	1
Bearnaise				
Made with Milk and Butter, 1 Cup (254.8g)	68	42	189	52
Béchamel				
Home Recipe, made with Butter, 1 Cup (255g)	24	7	145	15
Home Recipe, made with Margarine, 1 Cup (255g)	24	4	0	4
Cheese				
Made with Milk, 1 Cup (279.2g)	17	9	53	12
Chilli, Bottled				
1 Tbsp (15g)	0	0	0	0
1 Cup (273g)	1	0	0	0
Curry				
Made with Milk, 1 Cup (272.3g)	15	6	35	8
Guava				
1 Cup (238g)	0	0	0	0
Hollandaise				
Dry Mix with Butterfat, made with Water, 1 Cup (259.2g)	20	12	52	14
Dry Mix with Vegetable Oil, made with Milk and Butter, 1 Cup (254.8g)	68	42	189	52
Mushroom				
Dry Mix made with Milk, 1 Cup (266.7g)	10	5	35	7
Soubise				
Home Recipe, 1 Cup (255g)	24	7	145	15
Soured Cream				
Dry Mix made with Milk, 1 Cup (314.4g)	30	16	91	21
Soy				
1 Tbsp (18g)	0	0	0	0
1 Fl.oz (36g)	0	0	0	0
Spaghetti Sauce with Mushrooms				
1 Cup (200g)	4	2	11	3
Stroganoff				
Dry Mix made with Milk and Water, 1 Cup (296g)	11	7	39	9
Sweet and Sour				
Made with Water and Vinegar, 1 Cup (313.3g)	0	0	0	0

	TOTAL FAT (g)	SATURATED FAT (g)	CHOLES- TEROL (mg)	CQ
Tartar				
Low-cal, 10 Calories/tsp, 1 Tbsp (14g)	3	1	7	1
Regular, 1 Tbsp (14g)	8	2	7	2
1 Cup (230g)	133	25	117	31
Teriyaki				
Dry Mix made with Water, 1 Cup (283g)	1	0	0	0
Ready-to-serve, 1 Tbsp (18g)	0	0	0	0
1 Fl.oz (36g)	0	0	0	0
Tomato Ketchup, Bottled				
1 Tbsp (15g)	0	0	0	0
1 Cup (273g)	1	0	0	0
White				
Medium, 1 Cup (250g)	31	17	103	22
Thick, 1 Cup (250g)	39	21	125	28
Thin, 1 Cup (250g)	22	12	70	16
Dry Mix made with Milk, 1 Cup (263.8g)	14	6	34	8
Sauerkraut				
Juice, Tinned, 1 Cup (242g)	0	0	0	0
15oz Tin (453g)	0	0	0	0
Tinned, 1 Cup (236g)	0	0	0	0
Sausage Roll				
1 Sausage Roll (55g)	18	7	17	8

SAUSAGES

	TOTAL FAT (g)	SATURATED FAT (g)	CHOLES- TEROL (mg)	CQ
Berliner				
1 Slice (28.35g)	5	2	13	2
Bierwurst				
Beef, 1 Slice (23g)	7	3	14	4
Pork, 1 Slice (23g)	4	1	14	2
Black Pudding (Blood Sausage)				
1 Slice (28.35g)	10	4	34	6
Bockwurst				
1oz (28.35g)	8	3	17	4
1 Link (65g)	18	7	38	9
Bologna				
Beef, 1 Slice (28.35g)	8	3	16	4
Beef and Pork, 1 Slice (28.35g)	8	3	16	4
Pork, 1 Slice (28.35g)	6	2	17	3
Turkey, 1 Slice (28.35g)	4	1	28	3
Bratwurst				
1oz (28.35g)	7	3	17	4
1 Link (85g)	22	8	51	11
Braunschweiger				
Smoked, 1 Slice (28.35g)	9	3	44	5

	TOTAL FAT (g)	SATURATED FAT (g)	CHOLES-TEROL (mg)	CQ
Brawn				
1 Slice (28.35g)	5	1	23	3
Brotwurst				
1oz (28.35g)	8	3	18	4
1 Link (70g)	20	7	44	9
Capicola or Capacola				
1 Slice (21g)	10	4	14	4
Cervelas				
Dry, 4 Slices (12g)	5	2	8	2
Chorizo				
1oz (28.35g)	11	4	25	5
1 Link (60g)	23	9	53	11
Italian				
Cooked, 1 Link (83g)	21	8	65	11
Raw, 1 Link (113g)	35	13	86	17
Kielbasa (Kolbassy)				
1 Slice (28.35g)	8	3	19	4
Knackwurst				
1oz (28.35g)	8	3	16	4
1 Link (68g)	19	7	39	9
Liver Pudding				
1 Slice (28.35g)	7	3	49	5
Liver Sausage				
Smoked, 1 Slice (28.35g)	9	3	44	5
Liverwurst				
Raw, 1 Slice (28.35g)	8	3	45	5
Luncheon Type				
1 Slice (28.35g)	6	2	18	3
Meatless (Vegetarian)				
1 Link (25g)	5	1	0	1
Mortadella				
1 Slice (15g)	4	1	8	2
2 Slices (28.35g)	7	3	16	4
Pepperoni				
1 Slice (5.5g)	2	1	4	1
1 Sausage (251g)	110	41	198	51
Polish				
1 Slice (28.35g)	8	3	19	4
Polish-style				
1oz (28.35g)	8	3	20	4
1 Sausage (227g)	65	23	159	32
Pork and Beef				
1 Link (27g)	10	4	19	4
Pork Sausage Meat				
Cooked, 1 Link (27g)	8	3	22	4
Raw, 1 Link (57g)	23	8	39	10
Salami				
Beef and Pork, Cooked, 1 Slice (28.35g)	6	2	18	3

	TOTAL FAT (g)	SATURATED FAT (g)	CHOLES- TEROL (mg)	CQ
Beef and Pork, Dry, 1 Slice (10g)	3	1	8	2
Beef, Cooked, 1 Slice (28.35g)	6	3	18	3
Pork, Dry, 1 Slice (10g)	3	1	8	2
Smoked Sausage				
Pork, 1 Small Link (16g)	5	2	11	2
1 Large Link (68g)	22	8	46	10
Pork and Beef, 1 Small Link (16g)	5	2	11	2
1 Large Link (68g)	21	7	48	10
Thuringer				
1 Slice (28.35g)	8	3	21	5
Vienna				
Tinned, 1 Sausage (16g)	4	2	8	2
7 Sausages (113g)	29	11	59	14
Scone Dough				
Frozen, 3.5oz (100g)	12	3	0	3
Scone Mix				
Dry Mix, 1 Cup (128g)	16	4	0	4
Scones				
From Dry Mix, made with Milk, 1 Scone (28g)	3	1	0	1
Home Recipe, made with Lard, 1 Scone (28g)	5	2	5	2
Home Recipe, made with Vegetable Shortening, 1 Scone (28g)	5	1	0	1
Scotch Egg				
1 Scotch Egg (115g)	24	9	253	22
Scotch Pancakes				
4 Pancakes (170g)	69	8	85	12
Scrambled Eggs				
1 Large Egg (64g)	7	3	248	15
1 Cup (220g)	24	10	854	52
Seaweed				
Agar, Dried, 3.5oz (100g)	0	0	0	0
Agar, Fresh, 3.5oz (100g)	0	0	0	0
Dulse, Fresh, 3.5oz (100g)	3	0	0	0
Irishmoss, Fresh, 3.5oz (100g)	0	0	0	0
Kelp, Fresh, 3.5oz (100g)	1	0	0	0
Laver, Fresh, 3.5oz (100g)	0	0	0	0
Spirulina, Dried, 3.5oz (100g)	8	3	0	3
Spirulina, Fresh, 3.5oz (100g)	0	0	0	0
Wakame, Fresh, 3.5oz (100g)	1	0	0	0

SEEDS and SEED PRODUCTS

	TOTAL FAT (g)	SATURATED FAT (g)	CHOLES-TEROL (mg)	CQ
See also under Nut and Seed Butters, Nuts, Peanuts, Spices				
Breadfruit Seeds				
Boiled, 1oz (28.4g)	1	0	0	0
Fresh, 1oz (28.4g)	2	0	0	0
Roasted, 1oz (28.4g)	1	0	0	0
Cottonseed Kernels				
Roasted, 1 Tbsp (10g)	4	1	0	1
1 Cup (149g)	54	15	0	15
Cottonseed Meal				
Partially Defatted, 1oz (28.4g)	1	0	0	0
3.5oz (100g)	5	1	0	1
Lotus Seeds				
Dried, 1oz (28.4g)	1	0	0	0
1 Cup (32g)	1	0	0	0
Fresh, 1oz (28.4g)	0	0	0	0
Mustard Seeds				
Whole, Dried, 1oz (28.4g)	1	0	0	0
1 Cup (74g)	3	1	0	1
Pumpkin and Squash Seeds				
Kernels, Dried, 1oz (28.4g)	13	3	0	2
1 Cup (138g)	63	12	0	12
Kernels, Roasted, 1oz (28.4g)	12	2	0	2
1 Cup (227g)	96	18	0	18
Whole, Roasted, 1oz (28.4g)	6	1	0	1
1 Cup (64g)	12	2	0	2
Safflower Seed Kernels				
Dried, 1oz (28.4g)	11	1	0	1
Safflower Seed Meal				
Partially Defatted, 1oz (28.4g)	1	0	0	0
Sesame, Tahini				
From Fresh and Stone-Ground Kernels, 1oz (28.4g)	14	2	0	2
From Roasted and Toasted Kernels, 1oz (28.4g)	15	2	0	2
From Unroasted Kernels, 1oz (28.4g)	16	2	0	2
Sesame Meal				
Partially Defatted, 1oz (28.4g)	14	2	0	2
Sesame Paste				
1oz (28.4g)	14	2	0	2
Sesame Seeds				
Kernels, Dried, 1 Tbsp (8g)	4	1	0	1
1 Cup (150g)	82	12	0	12
Kernels, Toasted, 1oz (28.4g)	14	2	0	2
Whole, Dried, 1 Tbsp (9g)	5	1	0	1
1 Cup (144g)	72	10	0	10
Whole, Roasted and Toasted, 1oz (28.4g)	14	2	0	2
Dry, Decorticated, 1 Tbsp (8.0g)	4	1	0	1

	TOTAL FAT (g)	SATURATED FAT (g)	CHOLES- TEROL (mg)	CO
Sunflower Seed Butter				
1oz (28.4g)	14	1	0	1
Sunflower Seed Kernels				
Dried, 1oz (28.4g)	14	2	0	1
1 Cup (144g)	71	8	0	8
Dry Roasted, 1oz (28.4g)	14	2	0	1
1 Cup (128g)	64	7	0	7
Oil Roasted, 1oz (28.4g)	16	2	0	2
1 Cup (135g)	78	8	0	8
Toasted, 1oz (28.4g)	16	2	0	2
1 Cup (134g)	76	8	0	8
Watermelon Seed Kernels				
Dried, 1oz (28.4g)	14	3	0	3
1 Cup (108g)	51	11	0	11
Sesbania Flowers				
Fresh, 1 Cup Flowers (20g)	0	0	0	0
Steamed, 1 Cup Flowers (104g)	0	0	0	0
Shakes – *See* Milk Shakes				
Shallots				
Fresh, 1 Tbsp Chopped (10g)	0	0	0	0
Shellfish – *See under* Fish/shellfish				
Shepherd's Pie				
1 Serving (340g)	21	9	85	13
Snails				
Steamed or Boiled, 3oz (85g)	1	0	111	6
Raw, 3oz (85g)	0	0	55	3
Sorghum Grain				
All Types, 3.5oz (100g)	3	0	0	0

SOUP
Bean

	TOTAL FAT (g)	SATURATED FAT (g)	CHOLES- TEROL (mg)	CO
With Bacon, Dry Mix made with Water, 1 Cup (264.9g)	2	1	3	1
With Frankfurters, Tinned, Condensed, 1 Cup (263g)	14	4	24	5
1 Tin (319g)	17	5	29	7
With Frankfurters, Tinned, Diluted, 1 Cup (250g)	7	2	13	3
1 Tin (607g)	17	5	30	7

	TOTAL FAT (g)	SATURATED FAT (g)	CHOLES- TEROL (mg)	CQ
With Ham, Tinned, Chunky, Ready-to-serve,				
1 Cup (243g)	9	3	22	4
1 Tin (546g)	19	8	49	10
With Pork, Tinned, Condensed, 1 Cup (269g)	12	3	5	3
1 Tin (326g)	14	4	7	4
With Pork, Tinned, Diluted, 1 Cup (253g)	6	2	3	2
1 Tin (614g)	14	4	6	4
Beef				
Tinned, Chunky, Ready-to-serve, 1 Cup (240g)	5	3	14	3
1 Tin (539g)	12	6	32	7
Beef Broth				
Tinned, Condensed, 1 Cup (246g)	0	0	0	0
1 Tin (298g)	0	0	0	0
Tinned, Diluted, 1 Cup (241g)	0	0	0	0
1 Tin (586g)	0	0	0	0
Dry Mix made with Water, 1 Cup (244g)	1	0	0	0
Tinned, Ready-to-serve, 1 Cup (240g)	1	0	0	0
1 Tin (397g)	1	0	0	0
Beef Mushroom				
Tinned, Condensed, 1 Cup (251g)	6	3	13	4
1 Tin (305g)	7	4	15	4
Tinned, Diluted, 1 Cup (244g)	3	2	7	2
1 Tin (593g)	7	4	18	5
Beef Noodle				
Dry Mix made with Water, 1 Cup (251g)	1	0	3	0
Tinned, Condensed, 1 Cup (251g)	6	2	10	3
1 Tin (305g)	8	3	12	3
Tinned, Diluted, 1 Cup (244g)	3	1	5	1
1 Tin (593g)	8	3	12	3
Black Bean				
Tinned, Condensed, 1 Cup (257g)	3	1	0	1
1 Tin (312g)	4	1	0	1
Tinned, Diluted, 1 Cup (247g)	2	0	0	0
1 Tin (600g)	4	1	0	1
Cauliflower				
Dry Mix made with Water, 1 Cup (256.1g)	2	0	0	0
Cheese				
Tinned, Condensed, 1 Cup (257g)	21	13	59	16
1 Tin (312g)	25	16	72	20
Tinned, Prepared with Equal Volume Milk,				
1 Cup (251g)	15	9	48	12
1 Tin (609g)	35	22	116	28
Tinned, Prepared with Equal Volume Water,				
1 Cup (247g)	11	7	30	8
1 Tin (600g)	25	16	72	20

	TOTAL FAT (g)	SATURATED FAT (g)	CHOLES-TEROL (mg)	CQ
Chicken				
Tinned, Chunky, Ready-to-serve, 1 Cup (251g)	7	2	30	4
1 Tin (305g)	8	2	37	4
Chicken Broth or Bouillon				
Dry Mix made with Water, 1 Cup (244g)	1	0	0	0
Tinned, Condensed, 1 Cup (251g)	3	1	3	1
1 Tin (305g)	3	1	3	1
Tinned, Diluted, 1 Cup (244g)	1	0	0	0
1 Tin (593g)	3	1	0	1
Chicken Mushroom				
Tinned, Condensed, 1 Cup (251g)	18	5	20	6
1 Tin (305g)	22	6	24	7
Tinned, Diluted, 1 Cup (244g)	9	2	10	3
1 Tin (593g)	22	6	24	7
Chicken Noodle				
Dry Mix made with Water, 1 Cup (252.3g)	1	0	3	0
Tinned, Chunky, Ready-to-serve, 1 Cup (240g)	6	1	19	2
1 Tin (539g)	14	3	43	5
Tinned, Condensed, 1 Cup (246g)	5	1	12	2
1 Tin (298g)	6	2	15	2
Tinned, Diluted, 1 Cup (241g)	3	1	7	1
1 Tin (586g)	6	2	18	2
With Meatballs, Tinned, Chunky, Ready-to-serve,				
1 Cup (248g)	4	1	10	2
1 Tin (567g)	8	2	23	4
Chicken Rice				
Dry Mix made with Water, 1 Cup (252.8g)	1	0	3	0
Tinned, Chunky, Ready-to-serve, 1 Cup (240g)	3	1	12	2
1 Tin (539g)	7	2	27	4
Chicken Vegetable				
Dry Mix made with Water, 1 Cup (250.7g)	1	0	3	0
Tinned, Chunky, Ready-to-serve, 1 Cup (240g)	5	1	17	2
1 Tin (539g)	11	3	38	5
Tinned, Condensed, 1 Cup (246g)	6	2	17	3
1 Tin (298g)	7	2	21	3
Tinned, Diluted, 1 Cup (241g)	3	1	10	1
1 Tin (586g)	7	2	23	3
Chicken with Dumplings				
Tinned, Condensed, 1 Cup (246g)	11	3	66	6
1 Tin (298g)	13	3	81	7
Tinned, Diluted, 1 Cup (241g)	6	1	34	3
1 Tin (586g)	13	3	82	7
Chilli Beef				
Tinned, Condensed, 1 Cup (263g)	13	7	26	8
1 Tin (319g)	16	8	32	10
Tinned, Diluted, 1 Cup (250g)	7	3	13	4
1 Tin (607g)	16	8	30	10

	TOTAL FAT (g)	SATURATED FAT (g)	CHOLES- TEROL (mg)	CQ
Consommé				
With Gelatin, Dry Mix made with Water, 1 Cup (249g)	0	0	0	0
Crab				
Tinned, Ready-to-serve, 1 Cup (244g)	2	0	10	1
1 Tin (369g)	2	1	15	1
Cream of Asparagus				
Dry Mix made with Water, 1 Cup (250.8g)	2	0	0	0
Tinned, Condensed, 1 Cup (251g)	8	2	10	3
1 Tin (305g)	10	3	12	3
Tinned, Prepared with Equal Volume Milk, 1 Cup (248g)	8	3	22	4
1 Tin (602g)	20	8	54	11
Tinned, Prepared with Equal Volume Water, 1 Cup (244g)	4	1	5	1
1 Tin (593g)	10	3	12	3
Cream of Celery				
Dry Mix made with Water, 1 Cup (254g)	2	0	0	0
Tinned, Condensed, 1 Cup (251g)	11	3	28	4
1 Tin (305g)	14	3	34	5
Tinned, Prepared with Equal Volume Milk, 1 Cup (248g)	10	4	32	6
1 Tin (602g)	24	10	78	14
Tinned, Prepared with Equal Volume Water, 1 Cup (244g)	6	1	15	2
1 Tin (593g)	14	3	36	5
Cream of Chicken				
Dry Mix made with Water, 1 Cup (261.1g)	5	3	3	4
Tinned, Condensed, 1 Cup (251g)	15	4	20	5
1 Tin (305g)	18	5	24	6
Tinned, Prepared with Equal Volume Milk, 1 Cup (248g)	12	5	27	6
1 Tin (602g)	28	11	66	15
Tinned, Prepared with Equal Volume Water, 1 Cup (244g)	7	2	10	3
1 Tin (593g)	18	5	24	6
Cream of Mushroom				
Tinned, Condensed, 1 Cup (251g)	19	5	3	5
1 Tin (305g)	23	6	3	6
Tinned, Prepared with Equal Volume Milk, 1 Cup (248g)	14	5	20	6
1 Tin (602g)	33	13	48	15
Tinned, Prepared with Equal Volume Water, 1 Cup (244g)	9	2	2	3
1 Tin (593g)	22	6	6	6
Cream of Onion				
Tinned, Condensed, 1 Cup (251g)	11	3	30	4
1 Tin (305g)	13	4	37	5

	TOTAL FAT (g)	SATURATED FAT (g)	CHOLES- TEROL (mg)	CQ
Tinned, Prepared with Equal Volume Milk, 1 Cup (248g)	9	4	32	6
1 Tin (602g)	23	10	78	14
Tinned, Prepared with Equal Volume Water, 1 Cup (244g)	5	2	15	2
1 Tin (593g)	13	4	36	5
Cream of Potato				
Tinned, Condensed, 1 Cup (251g)	5	2	13	3
1 Tin (305g)	6	3	15	4
Tinned, Prepared with Equal Volume Milk, 1 Cup (248g)	6	4	22	5
1 Tin (602g)	16	9	54	12
Tinned, Prepared with Equal Volume Water, 1 Cup (244g)	2	1	5	1
1 Tin (593g)	6	3	12	4
Cream of Shrimp				
Tinned, Condensed, 1 Cup (251g)	10	7	33	8
1 Tin (305g)	13	8	40	10
Tinned, Prepared with Equal Volume Milk, 1 Cup (248g)	9	6	35	8
1 Tin (602g)	23	14	84	18
Tinned, Prepared with Equal Volume Water, 1 Cup (244g)	5	3	17	4
1 Tin (593g)	13	8	42	10
Cream of Tomato				
Home Made, 1 Serving (285g)	27	17	87	21
Cream of Vegetable				
Dry Mix made with Water, 1 Cup (260.1g)	6	1	0	1
Gazpacho				
Tinned, Ready-to-serve, 1 Cup (244g)	2	0	0	0
1 Tin (369g)	3	0	0	0
Irish Stew				
1 Serving (425g)	31	15	149	23
Leek				
Dry Mix made with Water, 1 Cup (253.9g)	2	1	3	1
Lentil with Ham				
Tinned, Ready-to-serve, 1 Cup (248g)	3	1	7	1
1 Tin (567g)	6	3	17	3
Minestrone				
Dry Mix made with Water, 1 Cup (253.9g)	2	1	3	1
Tinned, Condensed, 1 Cup (246g)	5	1	3	1
1 Tin (298g)	6	1	3	1
Tinned, Diluted, 1 Cup (241g)	3	1	2	1
1 Tin (586g)	6	1	6	2
Tinned, Chunky, Ready-to-serve, 1 Cup (240g)	3	2	5	2
1 Tin (539g)	6	3	11	4
Mushroom				
Dry Mix made with Water, 1 Cup (253g)	5	1	0	1

	TOTAL FAT (g)	SATURATED FAT (g)	CHOLES- TEROL (mg)	CQ
Mushroom Barley				
Tinned, Condensed, 1 Cup (251g)	5	1	0	1
1 Tin (305g)	6	1	0	1
Tinned, Diluted, 1 Cup (244g)	2	0	0	0
1 Tin (593g)	6	1	0	1
Mushroom with Beef Stock				
Tinned, Condensed, 1 Cup (251g)	8	3	15	4
1 Tin (305g)	10	4	18	5
Tinned, Diluted, 1 Cup (244g)	4	2	7	2
1 Tin (593g)	10	4	18	5
Onion				
Dry Mix made with Water, 1 Cup (246g)	1	0	0	0
Tinned, Condensed, 1 Cup (246g)	4	1	0	1
1 Tin (298g)	4	1	0	1
Tinned, Diluted, 1 Cup (241g)	2	0	0	0
1 Tin (586g)	4	1	0	1
Oxtail				
Dry Mix made with Water, 1 Cup (253.1g)	3	1	3	1
Oyster Stew				
Home Recipe, 1 Part Oysters to 2 Parts Milk, 1 Cup (240g)	15	7	86	12
Home Recipe, 1 Part Oysters to 3 Parts Milk, 1 Cup (240g)	13	7	70	11
Tinned, Condensed, 1 Cup (246g)	8	5	27	6
1 Tin (298g)	9	6	33	8
Tinned, Prepared with Equal Volume Milk, 1 Cup (245g)	8	5	32	7
1 Tin (595g)	19	12	77	16
Tinned, Prepared with Equal Volume Water, 1 Cup (241g)	4	3	15	3
1 Tin (586g)	9	6	35	8
Pea, Green				
Dry Mix made with Water, 1 Cup (271g)	2	0	3	1
Tinned, Condensed, 1 Cup (263g)	6	3	0	3
1 Tin (319g)	7	3	0	3
Tinned, Prepared with Equal Volume Milk, 1 Cup (254g)	7	4	18	5
1 Tin (616g)	17	10	43	12
Tinned, Prepared with Equal Volume Water, 1 Cup (250g)	3	1	0	1
1 Tin (607g)	7	3	0	3
Pea, Split Pea with Ham				
Tinned, Chunky, Ready-to-serve, 1 Cup (240g)	4	2	7	2
1 Tin (539g)	9	4	16	4
Tinned, Condensed, 1 Cup (269g)	9	4	16	4
1 Tin (326g)	11	4	20	5
Tinned, Diluted, 1 Cup (253g)	4	2	8	2
1 Tin (614g)	11	4	18	5

	TOTAL FAT (g)	SATURATED FAT (g)	CHOLES- TEROL (mg)	CQ
Scotch Broth				
Tinned, Condensed, 1 Cup (246g)	5	2	10	3
1 Tin (298g)	6	3	12	3
Tinned, Diluted, 1 Cup (241g)	3	1	5	1
1 Tin (586g)	6	3	12	3
Tomato				
Cream of, Home Recipe, 1 Serving (285ml)	27	17	87	21
Dry Mix made with Water, 1 Cup (265g)	2	1	0	1
Tinned, Condensed, 1 Cup (251g)	4	1	0	1
1 Tin (305g)	5	1	0	1
Tinned, Prepared with Equal Volume Milk, 1 Cup				
(248g)	6	3	17	4
1 Tin (602g)	15	7	42	9
Tinned, Prepared with Equal Volume Water,				
1 Cup (244g)	2	0	0	0
1 Tin (593g)	5	1	0	1
Tomato Beef with Noodle				
Tinned, Condensed, 1 Cup (251g)	9	3	8	4
1 Tin (305g)	10	4	9	4
Tinned, Diluted, 1 Cup (244g)	4	2	5	2
1 Tin (593g)	10	4	12	4
Tomato Bisque				
Tinned, Condensed, 1 Cup (257g)	5	1	10	2
1 Tin (312g)	6	1	13	2
Tinned, Prepared with Equal Volume Milk, 1 Cup				
(251g)	7	3	23	4
1 Tin (609g)	16	8	55	10
Tinned, Prepared with Equal Volume Water,				
1 Cup (247g)	3	1	5	1
1 Tin (600g)	6	1	12	2
Tomato Rice				
Tinned, Condensed, 1 Cup (257g)	5	1	3	1
1 Tin (312g)	7	1	3	1
Tinned, Diluted, 1 Cup (247g)	3	1	3	1
1 Tin (600g)	7	1	6	2
Tomato Vegetable				
Dry Mix made with Water, 1 Cup (253g)	1	0	0	0
Turkey Noodle				
Tinned, Condensed, 1 Cup (251g)	4	1	10	2
1 Tin (305g)	5	1	12	2
Tinned, Diluted, 1 Cup (244g)	2	1	5	1
1 Tin (593g)	5	1	12	2
Turkey Vegetable				
Tinned, Condensed, 1 Cup (246g)	6	2	3	2
1 Tin (298g)	7	2	3	2
Tinned, Diluted, 1 Cup (241g)	3	1	2	1
1 Tin (586g)	7	2	6	2

	TOTAL FAT (g)	SATURATED FAT (g)	CHOLES-TEROL (mg)	CO
Turkey				
Chunky, Ready-to-serve, 1 Cup (236g)	4	1	9	2
1 Tin (532g)	10	3	21	4
Vegetable				
Tinned, Chunky, Ready-to-serve, 1 Cup (240g)	4	1	0	1
1 Tin (539g)	8	1	0	1
Vegetarian, Tinned, Condensed, 1 Cup (246g)	4	1	0	1
1 Tin (298g)	5	1	0	1
Vegetarian, Tinned, Diluted, 1 Cup (241g)	2	0	0	0
1 Tin (586g)	5	1	0	1
Vegetable Beef				
Dry Mix made with Water, 1 Cup (253.1g)	1	1	0	1
Tinned, Condensed, 1 Cup (251g)	4	2	10	2
1 Tin (305g)	5	2	12	3
Tinned, Diluted, 1 Cup (244g)	2	1	5	1
1 Tin (593g)	5	2	12	3
Vegetable with Beef Broth				
Tinned, Condensed, 1 Cup (246g)	4	1	3	1
1 Tin (298g)	5	1	3	1
Tinned, Diluted, 1 Cup (241g)	2	0	2	1
1 Tin (586g)	5	1	6	1
Soured Cream				
1 Tbsp (12g)	3	2	5	2
1 Cup (230g)	48	30	102	35
Imitation, Non-dairy, Cultured, 1oz (28g)	6	5	0	5
1 Cup (230g)	45	41	0	41
Soursop				
Fresh, 1 Fruit (625g)	2	0	0	0
Soy Milk				
1 Cup (240g)	5	1	0	1
Soy Sauce				
1 Tbsp (18g)	0	0	0	0
¼ Cup (58g)	0	0	0	0
Spaghetti				
In Tomato Sauce with Cheese, Home Recipe, 1 Cup (250g)	9	2	8	2
In Tomato Sauce with Cheese, Tinned, 1 Cup (250g)	2	0	8	0
1 Tin (432g)	3	0	13	1
Noodles, Boiled, 1 Cup (140g)	1	0	0	0
And Meat Balls, in Tomato Sauce, Home Recipe, 1 Cup (248g)	12	3	74	7
1 Portion (537g)	25	7	161	15

	TOTAL FAT (g)	SATURATED FAT (g)	CHOLES-TEROL (mg)	CO
And Meat Balls, in Tomato Sauce, Tinned, 1 Cup				
(250g)	10	2	23	3
1 Tin (425g)	17	4	38	6

SPICES

	TOTAL FAT (g)	SATURATED FAT (g)	CHOLES-TEROL (mg)	CO
Allspice, Ground				
1 Tsp (1.9g)	0	0	0	0
1 Tbsp (6.0g)	1	0	0	0
Anise Seed				
1 Tsp (2.1g)	0	0	0	0
1 Tbsp (6.7g)	1	0	0	0
Basil, Ground				
1 Tsp (1.4g)	0	0	0	0
1 Tbsp (4.5g)	0	0	0	0
Bay Leaf, Crumbled				
1 Tsp (0.6g)	0	0	0	0
1 Tbsp (1.8g)	0	0	0	0
Caraway Seed				
1 Tsp (2.1g)	0	0	0	0
1 Tbsp (6.7g)	1	0	0	0
Cardamon, Ground				
1 Tsp (2.0g)	0	0	0	0
1 Tbsp (5.8g)	0	0	0	0
Celery Seed				
1 Tsp (2.0g)	1	0	0	0
1 Tbsp (6.5g)	2	0	0	0
Chervil, Dried				
1 Tsp (0.6g)	0	0	0	0
1 Tbsp (1.9g)	0	0	0	0
Chilli Powder				
1 Tsp (2.6g)	0	0	0	0
1 Tbsp (7.5g)	1	0	0	0
Cinnamon, Ground				
1 Tsp (2.3g)	0	0	0	0
1 Tbsp (6.8g)	0	0	0	0
Cloves, Ground				
1 Tsp (2.1g)	0	0	0	0
1 Tbsp (6.6g)	1	0	0	0
Coriander Leaf, Dried				
1 Tsp (0.6g)	0	0	0	0
1 Tbsp (1.8g)	0	0	0	0
Coriander Seed				
1 Tsp (1.8g)	0	0	0	0
1 Tbsp (5.0g)	1	0	0	0
Cumin Seed				
1 Tsp (2.1g)	1	0	0	0
1 Tbsp (6.0g)	1	0	0	0

	TOTAL FAT (g)	SATURATED FAT (g)	CHOLES-TEROL (mg)	CQ
Curry Powder				
1 Tsp (2.0g)	0	0	0	0
1 Tbsp (6.3g)	1	0	0	0
Dill Seed				
1 Tsp (2.1g)	0	0	0	0
1 Tbsp (6.6g)	1	0	0	0
Dill Weed, Dried				
1 Tsp (1.0g)	0	0	0	0
1 Tbsp (3.1g)	0	0	0	0
Fennel Seed				
1 Tsp (2.0g)	0	0	0	0
1 Tbsp (5.8g)	1	0	0	0
Fenugreek Seed				
1 Tsp (3.7g)	0	0	0	0
1 Tbsp (11.1g)	1	0	0	0
Garlic Granules or Powder				
1 Tsp (2.8g)	0	0	0	0
1 Tbsp (8.4g)	0	0	0	0
Ginger, Ground				
1 Tsp (1.8g)	0	0	0	0
1 Tbsp (5.4g)	0	0	0	0
Mace, Ground				
1 Tsp (1.7g)	1	0	0	0
1 Tbsp (5.3g)	2	1	0	1
Marjoram, Dried				
1 Tsp (0.6g)	0	0	0	0
1 Tbsp (1.7g)	0	0	0	0
Mustard Seed, Yellow				
1 Tsp (3.3g)	1	0	0	0
1 Tbsp (11.2g)	3	0	0	0
Nutmeg, Ground				
1 Tsp (2.2g)	1	1	0	1
1 Tbsp (7.0g)	3	2	0	2
Onion Powder				
1 Tsp (2.1g)	0	0	0	0
1 Tbsp (6.5g)	0	0	0	0
Oregano, Dried				
1 Tsp (1.5g)	0	0	0	0
1 Tbsp (4.5g)	1	0	0	0
Paprika				
1 Tsp (2.1g)	0	0	0	0
1 Tbsp (6.9g)	1	0	0	0
Parsley, Dried				
1 Tsp (0.3g)	0	0	0	0
1 Tbsp (1.3g)	0	0	0	0
Pepper				
Black, 1 Tsp (2.1g)	0	0	0	0
1 Tbsp (6.4g)	0	0	0	0

	TOTAL FAT (g)	SATURATED FAT (g)	CHOLES- TEROL (mg)	CO
Red or Cayenne, 1 Tsp (1.8g)	0	0	0	0
1 Tbsp (5.3g)	1	0	0	0
White, 1 Tsp (2.4g)	0	0	0	0
1 Tbsp (7.1g)	0	0	0	0
Poppy Seed				
1 Tsp (2.8g)	1	0	0	0
1 Tbsp (8.8g)	4	0	0	0
Poultry Seasoning				
1 Tsp (1.5g)	0	0	0	0
1 Tbsp (3.7g)	0	0	0	0
Rosemary, Dried				
1 Tsp (1.2g)	0	0	0	0
1 Tbsp (3.3g)	1	0	0	0
Saffron				
1 Tsp (0.7g)	0	0	0	0
1 Tbsp (2.1g)	0	0	0	0
Sage, Dried				
1 Tsp (0.7g)	0	0	0	0
1 Tbsp (2.0g)	0	0	0	0
Savory, Dried				
1 Tsp (1.4g)	0	0	0	0
1 Tbsp (4.4g)	0	0	0	0
Tarragon, Dried				
1 Tsp (1.6g)	0	0	0	0
1 Tbsp (4.8g)	0	0	0	0
Thyme, Dried				
1 Tsp (1.4g)	0	0	0	0
1 Tbsp (4.3g)	0	0	0	0
Turmeric, Ground				
1 Tsp (2.2g)	0	0	0	0
1 Tbsp (6.8g)	1	0	0	0
Spinach				
Boiled, 1 Cup (180g)	1	0	0	0
Fresh, 1 Cup Chopped (56g)	0	0	0	0
Soufflé, Home Recipe, 1 Cup (136g)	18	7	184	16
Tinned, 1 Cup (234g)	1	0	0	0
Sponge Cake				
1 Slice (55g)	15	5	72	9
Squab – See Pigeon				
Squash				
See also under Marrow, Pumpkin				
Acorn Squash				
Baked, 1 Cup Cubes (205g)	0	0	0	0
Boiled, 1 Cup Mashed (245g)	0	0	0	0

	TOTAL FAT (g)	SATURATED FAT (g)	CHOLES- TEROL (mg)	CQ
Fresh, 1 Cup Cubes (140g)	0	0	0	0
1 Squash, 4-in Diameter (431g)	0	0	0	0
Butternut Squash				
Baked, 1 Cup Cubes (205g)	0	0	0	0
Boiled, 1 Cup Mashed (240g)	0	0	0	0
Fresh, 1 Cup Cubes (140g)	0	0	0	0
Spaghetti Squash				
Boiled or Baked, 1 Cup (155g)	0	0	0	0
Fresh, 1 Cup Cubes (101g)	1	0	0	0
Summer Squash				
Boiled , 1 Cup Slices (180g)	1	0	0	0
Fresh, 1 Cup Slices (130g)	0	0	0	0
Starfruit, Fresh				
1 Fruit (127g)	0	0	0	0
Steak				
See also under Beef				
Flank, Grilled, 3oz (85g)	14	6	60	9
Gammon, Extra Lean, Grilled, 1 Slice (56.7g)	2	1	26	2
Porterhouse, Grilled, 3oz (85g)	18	8	71	11
Sirloin, Grilled, 3oz (85g)	15	6	77	10
T-bone, Grilled, 3oz (85g)	21	9	71	12
Tenderloin, Grilled, 3oz (85g)	15	6	72	10
Steak and Kidney Pie, Home Recipe				
1 Serving (170g)	31	13	213	23
Stock				
See also under Gravy, Soup				
Beef Stock Cube, Made with Water, 1 Cup (241.3g)	0	0	0	0
Chicken Stock Cube, Made with Water, 1 Cup (243g)	0	0	0	0
Dry Mix, Made with Water, 1 Cup (246.1g)	1	0	0	0
Tinned, 1 Cup (238.4g)	1	0	0	0
1 Tin (298g)	1	0	0	0
Strawberries				
Fresh, 1 Cup (149g)	1	0	0	0
1 Pint (320g)	1	0	0	0
Frozen, 1 Cup (255g)	0	0	0	0
Tinned, 1 Cup (254g)	1	0	0	0
Strawberry Flavour Beverage Mix				
Powder, 2–3 Heaping Tsp (21.6g)	0	0	0	0

	TOTAL FAT (g)	SATURATED FAT (g)	CHOLES- TEROL (mg)	CQ
Made with 1 Cup Milk and 2–3 Heaping Tsp Powder (266g)	8	5	32	7
Sugar				
Beet or Cane, Brown, 1 Cup (145g)	0	0	0	0
Beet or Cane, Granulated, 1 Tsp (4g)	0	0	0	0
1 Cup (200g)	0	0	0	0
Beet or Cane, Icing, 1 Cup (120g)	0	0	0	0
Swedes				
Boiled, 1 Cup Cubes (170g)	0	0	0	0
1 Cup Mashed (240g)	0	0	0	0
Fresh, 1 Cup Cubes (140g)	0	0	0	0
Sweetcorn				
Boiled, 1 Ear (77g)	1	0	0	0
Fresh, 1 Ear (90g)	1	0	0	0
Frozen Cob, Boiled, 1 Ear (63g)	1	0	0	0
Frozen Kernels, Boiled, 1 Cup (164g)	0	0	0	0
Tinned, Cream Style, 1 Cup (256g)	1	0	0	0
1 Tin (482g)	2	0	0	0
Tinned, Drained Solids, 1 Cup (164g)	2	0	0	0
1 Tin (298g)	3	1	0	0
Tinned, Solids and Liquid, 1 Cup (256g)	1	0	0	0
1 Tin (482g)	2	0	0	0
Tinned with Red and Green Peppers, 1 Cup (227g)	1	0	0	0
Sweet Potatoes				
Baked in Skin, 1 Sweetpotato (114g)	0	0	0	0
Boiled, without Skin, 1 Cup Mashed (328g)	1	0	0	0
Glazed, 1 Serving (105g)	3	1	8	2
Leaves, Fresh, 1 Cup Chopped (35g)	0	0	0	0
Leaves, Steamed, 1 Cup (64g)	0	0	0	0
Tinned, Mashed or Pieces, 1 Cup (255g)	1	0	0	0
1 Tin (496g)	1	0	0	0
Uncooked, 1 Sweetpotato (130g)	0	0	0	0

SWEETS
See also under Chocolate

	TOTAL FAT (g)	SATURATED FAT (g)	CHOLES- TEROL (mg)	CQ
Butterscotch				
1oz (28g)	1	1	3	1
Caramels				
Chocolate Flavoured, 1oz (28g)	3	1	0	1
Plain or Chocolate, 1oz (28g)	3	2	1	2
Plain or Chocolate with Nuts, 1oz (28g)	5	2	1	2

	TOTAL FAT (g)	SATURATED FAT (g)	CHOLES-TEROL (mg)	CQ
Chocolate-Coated Sweets				
Almonds, 1oz (28g)	12	2	0	2
1 Cup (165g)	72	12	2	12
Chocolate Fudge Centre, 1oz (28g)	5	2	1	2
Chocolate Fudge Centre with Nuts, 1oz (28g)	6	2	1	2
Coconut Centre, 1oz (28g)	5	3	0	3
Mint Fondant, 1 Large Mint (35g)	4	1	0	1
1 Small Mint (2.4g)	0	0	0	0
Fudge, Peanuts and Caramel Centre, 1oz (28g)	7	2	1	2
Hard Sweet Filled with Peanut Butter, 1oz (28g)	6	2	0	2
Nougat and Caramel, 1oz (28g)	4	1	1	1
Peanuts, 1oz (28g)	12	3	0	3
1 Cup (170g)	70	18	2	19
Raisins, 1oz (28g)	5	3	3	3
1 Cup (190g)	33	18	19	19
Vanilla Creams, 1oz (28g)	5	1	1	1
Chocolate				
Bitter, 1oz (28g)	11	6	0	6
Plain, 1oz (28g)	10	6	0	6
Sweet, 1oz (28g)	10	6	0	6
Fondant				
1 Cup (200g)	4	1	0	1
1 Cup Mints, Uncoated (110g)	2	1	0	1
Fudge				
Chocolate, 1oz (28g)	3	1	0	1
Chocolate, with Nuts, 1oz (28g)	5	1	0	1
Vanilla, 1oz (28g)	3	1	1	1
Vanilla, with Nuts, 1oz (28g)	5	1	1	1
Wine Gums				
1oz (28g)	0	0	0	0
Jelly Babies				
1oz (approx. 10) (28g)	0	0	0	0
1 Cup (approx. 75) (220g)	1	0	0	0
Marshmallows				
1 Large (7.2g)	0	0	0	0
1 Cup Miniature (46g)	0	0	1	0
Milk Chocolate				
Plain, 1oz (28g)	9	5	6	5
With Almonds, 1oz (28g)	10	5	5	5
With Peanuts, 1oz (28g)	11	4	4	5
Peanut Bars				
1oz (28g)	9	2	0	2
Peanut Brittle				
1oz (28g)	3	1	0	1
Rock				
1oz (28g)	0	0	0	0

	TOTAL FAT (g)	SATURATED FAT (g)	CHOLES- TEROL (mg)	CO
Sugar-coated Almonds				
1oz (28g)	5	0	0	0
1 Cup (195g)	36	3	0	3
Sugar-coated Chocolate Discs				
1oz (28g)	6	3	3	3
1 Cup (197g)	39	22	24	23
Syrup, Golden				
1 Cup (328g)	0	0	0	0
Taco				
With Meat Filling, Salad and Sauce, 1 Small				
(171g)	21	11	57	14
1 Large (263g)	32	17	87	22
Taco Salad				
With Chilli con Carne, 1½ Cups (261g)	13	6	4	6
Tahini (From Ground Sesame Seeds)				
1 Tbsp (15g)	7	1	0	1
1 Cup (227g)	109	15	0	15
Tamari				
1 Tbsp (18g)	0	0	0	0
¼ Cup (58g)	0	0	0	0
Tamarinds				
Fresh, 1 Fruit (2g)	0	0	0	0
1 Cup Pulp (120g)	1	0	0	0
Tangerines				
Fresh, 1 Fruit (84g)	0	0	0	0
1 Cup Sections (195g)	0	0	0	0
Tinned, 1 Cup (249g)	0	0	0	0
Tapioca Dessert				
1 Cup (250g)	0	0	0	0
Tapioca				
Dry, 1 Tbsp (8.4g)	0	0	0	0
1½ Cup (227g)	1	0	0	0
Taro				
Boiled or Baked, 1 Cup Slices (132g)	0	0	0	0
Fresh, 1 Cup Slices (104g)	0	0	0	0
Leaves, Fresh, 1 Cup (28g)	0	0	0	0
Leaves, Steamed, 1 Cup (145g)	1	0	0	0

	TOTAL FAT (g)	SATURATED FAT (g)	CHOLES-TEROL (mg)	CQ
Taro Chips				
1 Cup (10 Chips) (23g)	6	2	0	2
Tea				
Brewed, 6 Fl.oz (178g)	0	0	0	0
Herb, Brewed, 6 Fl.oz (178g)	0	0	0	0
Instant, Prepared, 1 Cup Water and 1 Tsp Powder (237g)	0	0	0	0
Tempeh				
1 Serving (83g)	6	1	0	1
1 Cup (166g)	13	2	0	2
Texturized Vegetable Protein (TVP), Dry				
1oz (28g)	1	0	0	0
1 Cup (88g)	3	0	0	0
Tofu				
Firm, 1 Serving (81g)	7	1	0	1
3.5oz (100g)	9	1	0	1
Freeze-dried, 1 Piece (17g)	5	1	0	1
3.5oz (100g)	30	4	0	4
Fried, 1 Slice (13g)	3	0	0	0
3.5oz (100g)	20	3	0	3
Okara, 1 Serving (61g)	1	0	0	0
3.5oz (100g)	2	0	0	0
Salted and Fermented, 1 Piece (11g)	1	0	0	0
3.5oz (100g)	8	1	0	1
Silken or Soft, 1 Serving (116g)	6	1	0	1
3.5oz (100g)	5	1	0	1
Tomato Juice				
Cocktail, Tinned or Bottled, 1 Cup (243g)	0	0	0	0
Tinned, 1 Cup (240g)	0	0	0	0
Tomato Ketchup, Bottled				
1 Tbsp (15g)	0	0	0	0
1 Cup (273g)	1	0	0	0
Tomato Paste, Tinned				
1 Tin (170g)	2	0	0	0
Tomato Purée, Tinned				
1 Cup (250g)	0	0	0	0
1 Tin (822g)	1	0	0	0

	TOTAL FAT (g)	SATURATED FAT (g)	CHOLES-TEROL (mg)	CO
Tomato Sauce				
Tinned, 1 Cup (245g)	0	0	0	0
Tinned or Bottled, for Spaghetti, 1 Cup (249g)	12	2	0	2
1 Jar (439g)	21	3	0	3
Tinned, Italian Style, 1 Cup (240g)	1	0	0	0
1 Tin (425g)	1	0	0	0
Tinned, with Herbs and Cheese, 1 Cup (240g)	5	2	0	2
1 Tin (425g)	8	3	0	3
Tinned, with Mushrooms, 1 Cup (245g)	0	0	0	0
Tinned, with Onions, 1 Cup (245g)	1	0	0	0
Tinned, with Onions, Green Peppers and Celery,				
1 Cup (240g)	2	0	0	0
1 Tin (411g)	3	1	0	1
Tinned, with Tomato Chunks, 1 Cup (240g)	1	0	0	0
1 Tin (425g)	2	0	0	0
Tomato Soup				
Cream of, Home Recipe, 1 Serving (285g)	27	17	87	21
Tomatoes				
Green, Fresh, 1 Tomato (123g)	0	0	0	0
Red, Ripe, Boiled, 1 Cup (240g)	1	0	0	0
Red, Fresh, 1 Tomato (123g)	0	0	0	0
1 Cup Chopped (180g)	0	0	0	0
Red, Tinned, Chopped in Tomato Juice, 1 Cup				
(261g)	0	0	0	0
Red, Tinned, Stewed, 1 Cup (255g)	0	0	0	0
Red, Tinned, Whole, 1 Cup (240g)	1	0	0	0
Tostada				
With Beans and Cheese, 1 Tostada (144g)	10	5	30	7
With Beans, Beef and Cheese, 1 Tostada (225g)	17	11	75	15
With Beef and Cheese, 1 Tostada (163g)	16	10	41	13
With Guacamole, 1 Tostada (131g)	12	5	20	6
With Salad and Cheese, 1 Tostada (144g)	11	5	18	6
Treacle				
1 Cup (328g)	0	0	0	0
Tripe				
Pickled, 3.5oz (100g)	1	1	68	4
Raw, 4oz (113g)	5	2	107	8

Trout – *See under* Fish/Shellfish

TURKEY

Dishes

	TOTAL FAT (g)	SATURATED FAT (g)	CHOLES- TEROL (mg)	CO
Diced and Seasoned, Light and Dark Meat				
1oz (28.35g)	2	1	16	1
1 Cup (227g)	14	4	125	10
Frozen Turkey and Gravy				
1 Cup (240g)	6	2	43	4
Luncheon Meat				
Cured, 1 Slice (28.4g)	1	1	16	2
Loaf, Breast Meat, 2 Slices (42.5g)	1	0	17	1
Patties, Breaded, Battered, Fried				
1 Regular Patty (64g)	12	3	40	5
1 Large Patty (94g)	17	4	58	7
Potted Turkey				
1 Tin (156g)	30	14	122	20
1 Cup (225g)	43	20	176	29
Pre-basted Breast, Meat and Skin, Roasted				
$\frac{1}{2}$ Breast (864g)	30	9	363	27
1 Breast (1728g)	60	17	726	53
Pre-basted Thigh, Meat and Skin, Roasted				
1 Thigh (314g)	27	8	195	18
2 Thighs (629g)	54	17	390	36
Pressed Breast Meat				
1 Slice (21g)	0	0	9	1
Sticks, Breaded, Battered, Fried				
1 Stick (64g)	11	3	41	5
2 Sticks (128g)	22	6	82	10
Tinned Turkey Meat with Broth				
1 Tin (142g)	10	3	94	8
Turkey Loaf				
1 Slice (28.35g)	4	1	28	3
Turkey Pastrami				
1 Slice (28.4g)	2	1	15	2
Turkey Pie				
Frozen, 3.5oz (100g)	10	4	9	4
Home Recipe, 1 Portion, $\frac{1}{3}$ of Pie (232g)	31	11	72	14
Turkey Roast				
Boneless, Frozen, Seasoned, Light and Dark Meat,				
Raw, 1 Portion (284g)	6	2	151	10
1 Roast (1134g)	25	8	601	38
Boneless, Frozen, Seasoned, Light and Dark Meat,				
Roasted, 1 Portion (196g)	11	4	104	9
1 Roast (782g)	45	15	415	36
Turkey Roll				
1 Slice (28.35g)	2	1	16	1

	TOTAL FAT (g)	SATURATED FAT (g)	CHOLES-TEROL (mg)	CQ
Turkey Salami				
1 Slice (28.4g)	4	1	23	2

Large Class
WHOLE BIRDS
Meat, Skin, Giblets and Neck

Roasted, 1 Turkey (4023g)	380	111	3822	304
Raw, 1 Turkey (5554g)	432	122	4332	340

Meat and Skin

Roasted, 1 Portion (240g)	23	7	197	17
½ Turkey (1857g)	181	53	1523	129
Raw, 1 Portion (332g)	27	8	226	19
½ Turkey (2565g)	206	58	1744	146

Meat Only

Roasted, 1 Portion (208g)	10	3	158	11
½ Turkey (1610g)	80	26	1231	88
Raw, 1 Portion (281g)	8	3	183	12
½ Turkey (2174g)	62	21	1413	92

Dark Meat and Skin

Roasted, 1 Portion (104g)	12	4	93	8
½ Turkey (808g)	93	28	719	64
Raw, 1 Portion (152g)	13	4	109	9
½ Turkey (1176g)	104	30	847	73

Dark Meat

Roasted, 1 Portion (91g)	7	2	77	6
½ Turkey (704g)	51	17	595	47
Raw, 1 Portion (132g)	6	2	91	7
½ Turkey (1017g)	45	15	702	50

Light Meat and Skin

Roasted, 1 Portion (136g)	11	3	103	8
½ Turkey (1050g)	88	25	798	65
Raw, 1 Portion (180g)	13	4	117	9
½ Turkey (1388g)	102	28	902	73

Light Meat

Roasted, 1 Portion (117g)	4	1	81	5
½ Turkey (906g)	29	9	628	41
Raw, 1 Portion (150g)	2	1	90	5
½ Turkey (1156g)	18	6	694	41

PART BIRDS
Back, Meat and Skin

Roasted, 1 Portion (34g)	5	1	31	3
½ Back (262g)	38	11	238	23
Raw, 1 Portion (47g)	6	2	35	3
½ Back (361g)	47	13	267	27

Breast, Meat and Skin

Roasted, 1 Portion (112g)	8	2	83	7
½ Breast (864g)	64	18	639	50

	TOTAL FAT (g)	SATURATED FAT (g)	CHOLES-TEROL (mg)	CQ
Raw, 1 Portion (146g)	10	3	95	8
½ Breast (1132g)	80	22	736	59
Giblets				
Simmered, with some Giblet Fat (145g)	7	2	606	33
Raw (244g)	10	3	688	38
Gizzard				
Simmered, 1 Cup (145g)	6	2	336	18
Raw, 1 Gizzard (113g)	4	1	179	10
Heart				
Simmered, 1 Cup (145g)	9	3	328	19
Raw, 1 Heart (29g)	2	1	33	2
Leg, Meat and Skin				
Roasted, 1 Portion (71g)	7	2	60	5
1 Leg (546g)	54	17	464	40
Raw, 1 Portion (105g)	7	2	75	6
1 Leg (816g)	55	17	579	46
Liver				
Simmered, 1 Cup (140g)	8	3	876	46
Raw, 1 Liver (102g)	4	1	475	25
Neck				
Meat Only, Simmered, 1 Neck (152g)	11	4	185	13
Meat Only, Raw, 1 Neck (180g)	10	3	142	10
Skin Only				
Roasted, 1 Portion (32g)	13	3	36	5
½ Turkey (248g)	98	26	280	40
Raw, 1 Portion (51g)	19	5	46	7
½ Turkey (392g)	145	38	357	56
Wing, Meat and Skin				
Roasted, 1 Wing (186g)	23	6	151	14
Raw, 1 Wing (256g)	32	8	179	17

Roasters
WHOLE BIRDS

	TOTAL FAT (g)	SATURATED FAT (g)	CHOLES-TEROL (mg)	CQ
Meat, Skin, Giblets and Neck				
Roasted, 1 Turkey (1772g)	100	29	2091	134
Raw, 1 Turkey (2410g)	102	29	2217	141
Meat and Skin				
Roasted, 1 Portion (229g)	13	4	241	16
½ Turkey (808g)	46	13	848	56
Raw, 1 Portion (310g)	13	4	251	16
½ Turkey (1093g)	47	13	885	58
Meat Only				
Roasted, 1 Portion (195g)	5	2	191	11
½ Turkey (687g)	18	6	676	40
Raw, 1 Portion (272g)	4	1	199	11
½ Turkey (960g)	15	5	701	40
Dark Meat and Skin				

	TOTAL FAT (g)	SATURATED FAT (g)	CHOLES- TEROL (mg)	CQ
Roasted, 1 Portion (106g)	8	2	124	8
½ Turkey (374g)	26	8	438	30
Raw, 1 Portion (151g)	7	2	131	9
½ Turkey (532g)	26	8	463	31
Dark Meat Only				
Roasted, 1 Portion (91g)	4	1	102	6
½ Turkey (320g)	14	5	359	23
Raw, 1 Portion (136g)	4	1	110	7
½ Turkey (479g)	13	4	388	24
Light Meat and Skin				
Roasted, 1 Portion (123g)	6	2	117	7
½ Turkey (433g)	20	5	411	26
Raw, 1 Portion (159g)	6	2	121	8
½ Turkey (561g)	21	6	426	27
Light Meat Only				
Roasted, 1 Portion (104g)	1	0	89	5
½ Turkey (367g)	4	1	317	17
Raw, 1 lb Ready To Cook Turkey (136g)	1	0	90	5
½ Turkey (481g)	2	1	318	17
PART BIRDS				
Back				
Roasted, 1 Portion (37g)	4	1	40	3
½ Back (130g)	13	4	140	11
Raw, 1 Portion (52g)	4	1	45	3
½ Back (183g)	13	4	157	12
Meat Only, Roasted, 1 Portion (27g)	2	1	26	2
½ Back (96g)	5	2	91	6
Meat Only, Raw, 1 Portion (43g)	2	1	32	2
½ Back (150g)	5	2	111	7
Breast				
Meat and Skin, Roasted, 1 Portion (98g)	3	1	88	5
½ Breast (344g)	11	3	310	19
Meat and Skin, Raw, 1 Portion (123g)	3	1	86	5
½ Breast (433g)	12	3	303	18
Meat Only, Roasted, 1 Portion (87g)	1	0	72	4
½ Breast (306g)	2	1	254	13
Meat Only, Raw, 1 Portion (111g)	1	0	69	4
½ Breast (390g)	3	1	242	13
Leg				
Meat and Skin, Roasted, 1 Portion (70g)	4	1	49	4
1 Leg (245g)	13	4	172	13
Meat and Skin, Raw, 1 Portion (99g)	4	1	86	5
1 Leg (349g)	13	4	304	19
Meat Only, Roasted, 1 Portion (64g)	2	1	76	5
1 Leg (224g)	8	3	267	16
Meat Only, Raw, 1 Portion (93g)	2	1	78	5
1 Leg (329g)	8	3	276	16

	TOTAL FAT (g)	SATURATED FAT (g)	CHOLES- TEROL (mg)	CO
Skin Only				
Roasted, 1 Portion (34g)	8	2	49	5
½ Turkey (121g)	28	7	174	16
Raw, 1 Portion (38g)	9	2	53	5
½ Turkey (133g)	31	8	185	17
Wing				
Meat and Skin, Roasted, 1 Portion (25g)	3	1	29	2
1 Wing (90g)	9	2	104	8
Meat and Skin, Raw, 1 Portion (36g)	3	1	35	3
1 Wing (128g)	10	3	125	9
Meat Only, Roasted, 1 Portion (17g)	1	0	17	1
1 Wing (60g)	2	1	61	4
Meat Only, Raw, 1 Portion (26g)	0	0	21	1
1 Wing (90g)	1	0	73	4

Young Cocks
WHOLE BIRDS

	TOTAL FAT (g)	SATURATED FAT (g)	CHOLES- TEROL (mg)	CO
Meat, Skin, Giblets and Neck				
Roasted, 1 Turkey (5957g)	525	154	5719	441
Raw, 1 Turkey (8399g)	606	172	6803	514
Meat and Skin				
Roasted, 1 Portion (239g)	22	6	196	16
½ Turkey (2750g)	249	73	2255	186
Raw, 1 Portion (338g)	25	7	243	19
½ Turkey (3895g)	289	82	2804	223
Meat Only				
Roasted, 1 Portion (206g)	10	3	159	11
½ Turkey (2376g)	111	37	1833	129
Raw, 1 Portion (286g)	8	3	195	12
½ Turkey (3302g)	89	29	2245	142
Dark Meat and Skin				
Roasted, 1 Portion (103g)	11	3	94	8
½ Turkey (1184g)	129	39	1077	93
Raw, 1 Portion (152g)	12	4	117	9
½ Turkey (1758g)	139	41	1354	109
Dark Meat Only				
Roasted, 1 Portion (90g)	6	2	79	6
½ Turkey (1033g)	72	24	907	70
Raw, 1 Portion (133g)	6	2	100	7
½ Turkey (1532g)	63	21	1149	79
Light Meat and Skin				
Roasted, 1 Portion (136g)	11	3	102	8
½ Turkey (1566g)	121	34	1175	93
Raw, 1 Portion (185g)	13	4	124	10
½ Turkey (2137g)	150	41	1432	113
Light Meat Only				
Roasted, 1 Portion (117g)	3	1	81	5
½ Turkey (1344g)	39	12	931	59

	TOTAL FAT (g)	SATURATED FAT (g)	CHOLES- TEROL (mg)	CQ
Raw, 1 Portion (154g)	2	1	96	6
½ Turkey (1771g)	28	9	1098	64

PART BIRDS
Back, Meat and Skin
Roasted, 1 Portion (33g)	5	1	31	3
½ Back (380g)	52	15	357	33
Raw, 1 Portion (45g)	5	1	36	3
½ Back (524g)	58	17	414	37

Breast
Meat and Skin, Roasted, 1 Portion (115g)	9	2	86	7
½ Breast (1329g)	98	28	997	78
Meat and Skin, Raw, 1 Portion (155g)	10	3	104	8
½ Breast (1789g)	113	31	1199	91

Leg
Meat and Skin, Roasted, 1 Portion (70g)	7	2	63	5
1 Leg (805g)	78	24	725	61
Meat and Skin, Raw, 1 Portion (107g)	7	2	81	6
1 Leg (1234g)	78	24	938	71

Skin Only
Roasted, 1 Portion (32g)	12	3	37	5
½ Turkey (374g)	139	36	438	59
Raw, 1 Portion (51g)	18	5	49	7
½ Turkey (592g)	205	53	562	82

Wing
Meat and Skin, Roasted, 1 Portion (21g)	2	1	17	2
1 Wing (237g)	27	7	192	17
Meat and Skin, Raw, 1 Portion (30g)	3	1	22	2
1 Wing (348g)	39	10	251	23

Young Hens
WHOLE BIRDS
Meat, Skin, Giblets and Neck
Roasted, 1 Turkey (3300g)	348	102	3102	258
Raw, 1 Turkey (4457g)	391	111	3254	275

Meat and Skin
Roasted, 1 Portion (243g)	26	8	190	17
½ Turkey (1524g)	166	49	1189	108
Raw, 1 Portion (327g)	30	8	206	19
½ Turkey (2052g)	187	53	1293	118

Meat Only
Roasted, 1 Portion (212g)	12	4	155	12
½ Turkey (1328g)	73	24	968	73
Raw, 1 Portion (276g)	9	3	166	11
½ Turkey (1731g)	55	18	1039	70

Dark Meat and Skin
Roasted, 1 Portion (106g)	14	4	89	9
½ Turkey (665g)	85	26	559	54

	TOTAL FAT (g)	SATURATED FAT (g)	CHOLES-TEROL (mg)	CQ
Raw, 1 Portion (152g)	16	5	99	10
½ Turkey (953g)	98	29	620	60
Dark Meat Only				
Roasted, 1 Portion (93g)	7	2	74	6
½ Turkey (580g)	45	15	460	38
Raw, 1 Portion (130g)	6	2	81	6
½ Turkey (812g)	40	13	503	39
Light Meat and Skin				
Roasted, 1 Portion (137g)	13	4	101	9
½ Turkey (859g)	81	23	636	55
Raw, 1 Portion (175g)	14	4	109	9
½ Turkey (1099g)	89	24	681	58
Light Meat Only				
Roasted, 1 Portion (119g)	5	1	81	5
½ Turkey (748g)	28	9	507	34
Raw, 1 Portion (147g)	2	1	85	5
½ Turkey (919g)	15	5	533	32
PART BIRDS				
Back				
Meat and Skin, Roasted, 1 Portion (35g)	6	2	30	3
½ Back (217g)	34	10	185	19
Meat and Skin, Raw, 1 Portion (47g)	8	2	32	4
½ Back (298g)	48	13	203	23
Breast				
Meat and Skin, Roasted, 1 Portion (109g)	9	3	79	6
½ Breast (686g)	54	15	494	40
Meat and Skin, Raw, 1 Portion (139g)	12	3	86	7
½ Breast (874g)	73	20	542	47
Leg				
Meat and Skin, Roasted, 1 Portion (71g)	8	2	58	5
1 Leg (448g)	47	15	367	33
Meat and Skin, Raw, 1 Portion (105g)	8	2	66	6
1 Leg (656g)	49	15	413	36
Skin Only				
Roasted, 1 Portion (31g)	14	4	33	5
½ Turkey (196g)	87	23	208	33
Raw, 1 Portion (51g)	21	5	41	8
½ Turkey (321g)	130	34	260	47
Wing				
Meat and Skin, Roasted, 1 Portion (28g)	4	1	22	2
1 Wing (174g)	23	6	134	13
Meat and Skin, Raw, 1 Portion (36g)	5	1	23	3
1 Wing (224g)	31	8	146	16
Turnip Greens				
Boiled, 1 Cup Chopped (180g)	0	0	0	0
Fresh, 1 Cup Chopped (55g)	0	0	0	0

	TOTAL FAT (g)	SATURATED FAT (g)	CHOLES- TEROL (mg)	CQ
Turnips				
Boiled, 1 Cup Cubes (156g)	0	0	0	0
1 Cup Mashed (230g)	0	0	0	0
Fresh, 1 Cup Cubes (130g)	0	0	0	0
Turtle, Green				
Raw, 3.5oz (100g)	1	0	50	3
Tinned, 3.5oz (100g)	1	0	50	3

VEAL

Composite Cuts
Fat Class

	TOTAL FAT (g)	SATURATED FAT (g)	CHOLES- TEROL (mg)	CQ
Raw (excluding Kidney and Kidney Fat), 3.5oz (100g)	16	8	71	11
Raw (including Kidney and Kidney Fat), 3.5oz (100g)	19	9	71	13
Medium-fat Class				
Raw (excluding Kidney and Kidney Fat), 3.5oz (100g)	12	6	71	9
Raw (including Kidney and Kidney Fat), 3.5oz (100g)	14	7	71	10
Thin Class				
Raw (excluding Kidney and Kidney Fat), 3.5oz (100g)	8	4	71	7
Raw (including Kidney and Kidney Fat), 3.5oz (100g)	10	5	71	8

Parts
Best End

	TOTAL FAT (g)	SATURATED FAT (g)	CHOLES- TEROL (mg)	CQ
Fat Class, Raw, 3.5oz (100g)	15	7	71	11
Medium-fat Class, Grilled, 1 Portion (90g)	12	6	91	11
Medium-fat Class, Raw, 3.5oz (100g)	11	5	71	9
Thin Class, Raw, 3.5oz (100g)	8	4	71	7
Fillet				
Fat Class, Raw, 3.5oz (100g)	12	6	71	9
Medium-fat Class, Grilled, 1 Portion (82g)	9	4	83	9
Medium-fat Class, Raw, 3.5oz (100g)	9	4	71	8
Thin class, Raw, 3.5oz (100g)	6	3	71	6
Flank (Tendron)				
Fat Class, Raw, 3.5oz (100g)	36	17	71	21
Medium-fat Class, Stewed, 3.5oz (100g)	32	16	101	21
Medium-fat Class, Raw, 3.5oz (100g)	27	13	71	17
Thin Class, Raw, 3.5oz (100g)	18	9	71	12
Foreshank				
Fat Class, Raw, 3.5oz (100g)	10	5	71	8

	TOTAL FAT (g)	SATURATED FAT (g)	CHOLES- TEROL (mg)	CQ
Medium-fat Class, Stewed, 3.5oz (100g)	10	5	101	10
Medium-fat Class, Raw, 3.5oz (100g)	8	4	71	7
Thin Class, Raw, 3.5oz (100g)	5	2	71	6
Middle Neck				
Fat Class, Raw, 3.5oz (100g)	19	9	71	13
Medium-fat Class, Roasted, 1 Portion (80g)	14	7	81	11
Medium-fat Class, Raw, 3.5oz (100g)	14	7	71	10
Thin Class, Raw, 3.5oz (100g)	9	4	71	8
Scrag End				
Fat Class, Raw, 3.5oz (100g)	23	11	71	15
Medium-fat Class, Stewed, 1 Portion (79g)	17	8	80	12
Medium-fat Class, Raw, 3.5oz (100g)	17	8	71	12
Thin Class, Raw, 3.5oz (100g)	12	6	71	9
Shoulder				
Fat Class, Raw, 3.5oz (100g)	13	6	71	10
Medium-fat Class, Braised, 1 Portion (80g)	10	5	81	9
Medium-fat Class, Raw, 3.5oz (100g)	10	5	71	8
Thin Class, Raw, 3.5oz (100g)	6	3	71	6
Veal Escalopes à la Viennoise (Wiener Schnitzel)				
1 serving, 3oz (85g)	28	11	137	18
VegeBurger				
Meatless Burger, Grilled or Baked, 1 Patty	10	0	0	0
Vegetable Juice Cocktail				
Tinned, 1 Cup (240g)	0	0	0	0
Vegetable Oyster				
Fresh, 1 Cup Slices (133g)	0	0	0	0
Vegetable Protein (TVP), Dry				
1oz (28g)	1	0	0	0
1 Cup (88g)	3	0	0	0
Vegetables				
See also under individual entries				
Mixed, Frozen Boiled, 1 Cup (182g)	0	0	0	0
Mixed, Tinned, 1 Cup (245g)	1	0	0	0
Vegetarian Bacon Substitute				
1 Strip (8g)	2	0	0	0
1 Cup Pieces (144g)	43	7	0	7
Vegetarian Meat, Tinned				
Peanuts and Soya, 3.5oz (100g)	17	4	0	4
Wheat and Soy Protein, 3.5oz (100g)	1	0	0	0

	TOTAL FAT (g)	SATURATED FAT (g)	CHOLES-TEROL (mg)	CQ
Wheat and Soy Protein, Soy and Other Vegetable Oils, 3.5oz (100g)	6	1	0	1
Wheat Protein, 3.5oz (100g)	1	0	0	0
Wheat Protein, Nuts or Peanuts, 3.5oz (100g)	7	2	0	2
Wheat Protein, Vegetable Oil, 3.5oz (100g)	10	3	0	3
Vegetarian Sausage, Meatless				
1 Link (25g)	5	1	0	1
1 Patty (38g)	7	1	0	1
Venison				
Lean Meat Only, Raw, 3oz (85g)	3	2	55	5
Vinegar				
Cider, 1 Tbsp (15g)	0	0	0	0
1 Cup (240g)	0	0	0	0
Distilled, 1 Tbsp (15g)	0	0	0	0
1 Cup (240g)	0	0	0	0
Waffle Mix				
Dry Form, 3.5oz (100g)	19	4	0	4
Plain and Buttermilk, Dry, 1 Cup (147g)	3	0	0	0
Waffles				
Home Recipe, 1 Waffle, 9-in Square (200g)	20	6	250	19
Made from Mix with Water, 3.5oz (100g)	14	3	0	3
Frozen, 1 Waffle (34g)	2	1	43	3
Waterchestnuts				
Tinned, 4 Waterchestnuts (28g)	0	0	0	0
½ Cup Slices (70g)	0	0	0	0
Fresh, 4 Waterchestnuts (36g)	0	0	0	0
½ Cup Slices (62g)	0	0	0	0
Watercress				
Fresh, 1 Cup Chopped (34g)	0	0	0	0
Watermelon				
Fresh, 1 Cup Diced Pieces (160g)	1	0	0	0
1 Slice, 10-in Diameter (482g)	2	0	0	0
Welsh Rarebit				
1 Serving (232g)	32	17	100	22
Whale Meat				
Raw, 3.5oz (100g)	8	1	50	4

	TOTAL FAT (g)	SATURATED FAT (g)	CHOLES- TEROL (mg)	CQ
Wheat				
Whole Grain, 3.5oz (100g)	2	0	0	0
Whole Grain, Durum, 3.5oz (100g)	3	0	0	0
Wheat Bran				
Crude, 3.5oz (100g)	5	1	0	1
Wheat Flour – *See under* Flour				
Wheat Germ				
Crude, 3.5oz (100g)	11	2	0	2
Whey				
Acid, Dried, 1 Tbsp (2.9g)	0	0	0	0
1 Cup (57g)	0	0	2	0
Acid, Fluid, 1 Cup (246g)	0	0	1	0
Sweet, Dried, 1 Tbsp (7.5g)	0	0	1	0
1 Cup (145g)	2	1	9	1
Sweet, Fluid, 1 Cup (246g)	1	1	5	1
Wiener Schnitzel				
1 serving, 3oz (85g)	28	11	137	18
Wild Rice				
Uncooked, 1 Cup (160g)	1	0	0	0
Wine – *See under* Alcohol				
Yam				
Boiled or Baked, 1 Cup Cubes (136g)	0	0	0	0
Fresh, 1 Cup Cubes (150g)	0	0	0	0
Yeast				
Baker's, Compressed, 1oz (28g)	0	0	0	0
Baker's, Dry, Active, 1oz (28g)	0	0	0	0
Brewer's, Debittered, 1oz (28g)	0	0	0	0
Yeast Extract				
1oz (28g)	0	0	0	0
Yoghurt				
Fruit, Low-fat, 1 Small Container (113g)	2	1	6	1
1 Medium Container (227g)	3	2	13	3
Plain, Low-fat, 1 Small Container (113g)	2	1	7	1
1 Medium Container (227g)	4	2	14	3
Plain, Skimmed Milk, 1 Small Container (113g)	0	0	2	0
1 Medium Container (227g)	0	0	4	0

	TOTAL FAT (g)	SATURATED FAT (g)	CHOLES- TEROL (mg)	CO
Plain, Whole Milk, 1 Small Container (113g)	4	2	14	3
1 Medium Container (227g)	7	5	29	6
Vanilla, Low-fat, 1 Small Container (113g)	1	1	6	1
1 Medium Container (227g)	3	2	11	2
Yorkshire Pudding				
2 Puddings (55g)	6	3	39	4

APPENDIX I

TRACKING YOUR FAT

The Quick Cholesterol and Fat Counter™ can also help you to keep track of your fat intake. This is just as important – many experts would say *more* important – than counting calories, because fat is the greatest single source of calories in our diets. Excess fat in the diet can make you put on weight, leading to obesity, and is also a major factor in the development of many diseases. You can simply check the total fat content of any food you intend to buy or eat by looking at the first column of figures (headed 'Total Fat') in the tables, and adding them up.

SATURATED FAT AND CHOLESTEROL
Saturated fat in the diet increases the amount of cholesterol in your blood, and should be reduced wherever possible. Saturated fat is usually solid when at room temperature, and includes animal fats such as lard, dripping and butter, and also the fats from the coconut and palm plants. Saturated fat doesn't only appear in solid blocks, however. It is also present in meat, milk and eggs, and there are also small amounts in some vegetable foods.

To minimize the amount of fat you include in your diet, select only those fats which in some way enhance your health. For instance, olive oil and oils high in linoleic acid (e.g. safflower oil) are beneficial to the transportation of fatty acids and fat-soluble vitamins. Used in small amounts, they provide the flavour and 'body' that is often desired in a meal.

Although individual figures for saturated fat and cholesterol content of foods are given in the tables, this is for the sake of completeness: there is usually little need to keep a separate total of these amounts because both figures have been combined into the 'Cholesterol Quotient', as explained in the introduction.

APPENDIX II

HOW 'CHOLESTEROL QUOTIENTS' HAVE BEEN CALCULATED

'Cholesterol Quotients' have been calculated using the Cholesterol/ Saturated Fat Index formula, produced by researchers working at the Oregon Health Sciences University[1] as a method of measuring a food's potential to raise cholesterol levels in the blood and, thus, to contribute to the build-up of atheroma. It is based on a regression equation computed from metabolic studies designed to lower plasma lipids. A low CSI indicates low saturated fat and cholesterol content and low atherogenicity.

CQ limits have been calculated as follows:

CQ Limit 1: For the general population
Maximum saturated fat intake = 10 per cent of calories; maximum dietary cholesterol = 300 mg per day. Average Kcal intake taken as 2300 per day for all calculations.

CQ Limit 2: For those with some risk factors
Guidelines put forward by the (US) National Cholesterol Education Program and the US Surgeon General[2] suggest that adults with total cholesterol levels of 240 mg/dl or above and those with total cholesterol levels of 200 to 239 mg/dl with coronary heart disease (CHD) or two or more CHD risk factors should reduce intake of total fat to less than 30 per cent of calories, saturated fat to less than 10 per cent of calories, and dietary cholesterol to less than 300 mg per day. The guidelines applying to total and saturated fat intake were also suggested by the World Health Organization[3]. To stay within these limits, maximum saturated fat intake has been calculated as 8 per cent of calories, and maximum dietary cholesterol at 200 mg per day.

[1] For a complete explanation of the CSI, consult Connor, S. L. et al., 'The cholesterol/ saturated-fat index: an indication of the hypercholesterolaemic and atherogenic potential of food', Lancet, 31 May 1986, 1 (8492) pp. 1229–32.

[2] 'The Surgeon General's Report on Nutrition and Health', US Department of Health and Human Services, 1988.

[3] 'Prevention of Coronary Heart Disease', WHO technical report series no. 678.

156

CQ Limit 3: For those with a greater need to lower cholesterol

The National Cholesterol Education Program suggests that if cholesterol lowering is insufficient after three months on the above regime, saturated fat should be further reduced to less than 7 per cent of calories and cholesterol intake to less than 200 mg per day. To stay within these limits, maximum saturated fat intake has been calculated as 5 per cent of calories, and maximum dietary cholesterol at 140 mg per day.

HOW TO WRITE TO US

Peter Cox and Peggy Brusseau can't advise on specific health problems, but would be pleased to know your comments on this book. They also produce *The Whole Family Newsletter*, which keeps its readers abreast of developments in many exciting areas. If you wish to write to them, or want to receive details about *The Whole Family Newsletter*, please send a stamped self-addressed envelope to:

The Whole Family
PO Box 1612
London NW3 1TD